LUNCHBOX

BRIGHT IDEAS FOR MOVEABLE FEASTS

TV cook and food writer Amanda Grant is a presenter on Channel 4's *Here's One I Made Earlier*. She also appears on the BBC's *Food & Drink* programme. Amanda is food editor for *Cosmopolitan* and writes a weekly food column for the *Sunday Mirror* magazine. She is also the author of the *Cosmopolitan Vegetarian Cookbook*.

LUNCHBOX

BRIGHT IDEAS FOR MOVEABLE FEASTS

AMANDA GRANT

PRION

First published in 1999 by
Prion Books Limited, Imperial Works,
Perren Street, London NW5 3ED

Reprinted 1999 twice and 2000 twice

ISBN 1-85375-314-9

Cover design by Jamie Keenan
Printed and bound in Singapore
by Kyodo Printing Pte

CONTENTS

Acknowledgements

For David, thank you for all your love and support. You are an excellent chief tester, but I am concerned about the weight gain – you are only supposed to 'taste'!

Billy, thank you so much for all your hard work, I hope you still enjoy sandwiches and salads after all that testing!

Kirsten, your 'Le Pont de la Tour food store' is a joy to spend time in, I always leave with inspiration and I really appreciate all your enthusiastic ideas.

Thanks to Andrew at Prion for commissioning me to write this book and to Catherine for all your fabulous tasting compliments.

I am grateful to all the people who helped with research and kept me up-to-date with all the latest products to hit the shop shelves.

Thanks to Paul Heathcote, you are a star!

INTRODUCTION

The recipes in *Lunchbox* are versatile meals that can be taken or eaten anywhere
– delicious food that can be enjoyed at school, work, on a picnic or at home
with friends.

There are quick ideas for those of you who are short of time, as well as a
selection of recipes that can be prepared at the same time as you make supper.

If you are looking for an inspirational sandwich filling or a different salad,
there are many new ideas to choose from. For those of you interested in
vegetarian ideas or ways to reduce your fat intake, there are examples of
both throughout each section.

Where necessary I have included tips on storage to help your lunchbox
stay in perfect condition until you are ready to eat.

I hope these recipes will tempt you to make exciting changes to your normal
lunches, whether you are preparing food for yourself, your children or for a
group of friends. If you are transporting the food invest in a few new funky
plastic boxes and flasks...

Lunchtime need never be the same again.

ESSENTIAL INGREDIENTS

You can buy the following ingredients in large supermarkets, local delis or organic food stores. Try and support local organic producers when ever possible. On that note, I strongly advise you to buy organic foods and take advantage of the fabulous array of organic ingredients now available to us. Whatever your personal beliefs for eating organic food, be it for health, fewer pesticide residues, taste, the idea that organic food has a higher nutritional value, the concern for the environment or animal welfare, you are sure to notice a difference. I have not specified which of the following ingredients are organic as I am hoping that you will always look for the organic option. Use this list as a guide to the sort of foods to keep in the cupboard, fridge and freezer so that you never get caught short.

STORE CUPBOARD

Fresh bread: keep a loaf or rolls of fresh bread and you will always be able to make a sandwich. Also, if you keep a selection of breads (including part baked) in the freezer you will never get caught out.

Couscous: these tiny grains of semolina coated in wheat flour are so quick and easy to use. Just as versatile as rice, couscous makes a perfect accompaniment to almost any salad ingredient.

Basmati rice: easy to use and quick to cook; you will always have a lunch if you have cooked rice. Just add anything else from your fridge such as tomatoes, cooked chicken and a few vegetables. Always keep the rice chilled and never reheat.

Egg noodles and rice noodles: these are very quick to prepare and can be transformed into delicious salads.

Nuts and seeds: both pumpkin and sunflower seeds are easy to use; toasted and tossed with spices they make a great addition to any lunchbox.

Canned foods: chick peas, cannellini beans, butter beans, puy lentils and sweetcorn are my favourite canned vegetables. Give these a good rinse under the tap before using them to wash off any sugar or salt in their water. Canned tomatoes are essential. There are only a few other ingredients that work really well in tins – coconut milk and tuna being two good examples. For quick sweet snack attacks, canned creamed rice pudding (with lashings of syrup) does the trick!

Sauces: chutneys, wholegrain mustards, olive paste, pesto, harissa, dark and light soy sauces. Harissa is particularly good tossed through couscous and roasted vegetables.

Jars: jars of roasted peppers, artichokes or aubergines are not really essential, more of a luxury, but they are incredibly useful and very tasty.

Oils: if you have the space for more than just one, go for a light olive oil, and an extra virgin which is great for salad dressings and drizzling over lightly cooked vegetables or finished dishes (although I must confess I do tend to use extra virgin for everything). If you find yourself with fresh bread and nothing to put on it, a rub of garlic and a drizzle of extra virgin olive oil is simply scrumptious.

Vinegars: balsamic is essential, but you need to spend a little to get a good, dark, sweet and rich yet mellow flavour. Rice wine vinegar is a must: I remember when you needed time and patience to find this little ingredient but now all you need to do is pop into the nearest supermarket. Cider vinegar and red wine vinegar are also worth keeping.

Seasonings and spices: my advice is to keep a few whole spices – such as green cardamom pods, coriander seeds, black peppercorns, cinnamon sticks and dried chillies – and grind them as and when required. Vanilla pods are nice to have for those quick custards or to scrape out the seeds for mixing into crème fraîche. Dried orange or lime zest ground in your pepper mill makes a wonderful fresh seasoning. Sea salt flakes have such a wonderful taste of the sea that you will find you need to use less than normal salt.

Preserves: fruit jams with a high fruit content and little sugar and a good runny honey. Pickled ginger is the most convenient form of that wonderful Japanese ingredient that adds a kick to food, but watch out for the bright pink kind – the colour indicates the presence of a nasty dye.

Sugars: unrefined sugars are the only ones to use. I will never make any puddings, biscuits, cakes or meringues without this essential ingredient ever again. Always check that the label stays the sugar is unrefined, otherwise you may be buying a white sugar that has been coloured brown. A spoonful of Muscovado sugar or golden icing sugar mixed with yoghurt can only be described as gooey fudge on a spoon!

Wasabi: it may look like a squeezy tube of toothpaste but don't be fooled. Squeeze it into a little pot and use with caution – it is Japanese horseradish with a real attitude.

FRIDGE

Cheese: a couple of good and versatile cheeses such as Cheddar, Parmesan, ricotta, Gorgonzola, Gruyère, mascarpone, mozzarella, Fontina and goat's cheese. Experiment with different cheeses as very often they are interchangeable.

Crème fraîche and yoghurt: always useful ingredients. They make a good base for dips or dreamy desserts swirled with a good-quality fruit jam or puréed fresh fruit.

Green leaves: a packet of fresh rocket or watercress.

Fresh herbs: do try to keep a few growing in your kitchen. A handful of fresh herbs adds aroma, colour and flavour to a dish that cannot be achieved so simply and effectively by any other ingredient.

Chillies: as a general guide, skinny chillies are hotter than those with broad shoulders, although the scotch bonnet proves otherwise. Add a little at a time and taste as you go – you can always add more if necessary. As soon as you add an ingredient like coconut milk or any other high-fat liquid to chilli or chilli paste the taste will become milder. Another interesting fact is that fresh chillies with wrinkled skins are hotter than the smooth kind. (This is the exact opposite with dried: if dried chillies are wrinkled they are often sweeter than the smooth, hotter ones.)

Salsa and humus: you will never be caught lunchless if you have a part-baked bread in your freezer and a salsa in your fridge.

FREEZER

Part-baked breads and rolls: bake these for sandwiches or to take in chunks with a selection of cheeses or pâtés.

Berries: a bag of frozen berries is always handy. Defrost and mix with yoghurt or make an Eton mess (see page 262). Alternatively, poach the fruit gently and turn it into a sauce for serving with biscuits or yoghurts.

QUICK NIBBLES

For days when all you want to do is nibble, here are some very quick and easy recipes for food that can be munched on any time, anywhere. There are also fun ideas here to help pad out the lunchbox with something more interesting than the usual packet of crisps. Choose anything from Cajun sticky chicken wings, olives with rosemary and feta, spicy mushrooms, or sausages with soy and marmalade.

HOT AND SPICY POPCORN

A wonderful idea for children's packed lunches, healthier than lots of crisps and they'll love eating popcorn tossed in different seasonings. Fill little sandwich bags from the big batch you've made, they will last for a couple of days, if kept airtight. It's important to use a heavy-based saucepan or frying pan with a tight-fitting lid. Experiment with other seasonings of your choice. For sweet popcorn simply replace the seasoning and spices with sugar and cinnamon.

SERVES 4, PREP 10 MINS, COOKING 10 MINS

1 tbsp vegetable oil
125 g / 4 oz corn kernels
2 tbsp olive oil

sea salt flakes, ground black pepper,
cayenne pepper and paprika, to taste

Heat the vegetable oil until hot. Add the kernels in a single layer, then cover the pan. Listen to the pan and when the kernels begin to pop, turn the heat down and shake gently. When the popping stops, take the pan from the heat. Allow to cool slightly. Add the olive oil and seasoning, cayenne pepper and paprika to taste. Toss the popcorn gently in the pan, then either turn into a serving dish or allow to cool and transfer to an airtight container until you are ready to eat it.

OLIVES WITH ROSEMARY AND FETA

Why pay through the nose for a little serving of marinated olives when you can add some fresh herbs and cheese to a pot of your own? Just remember to take a napkin to work with you. As an alternative, substitute a couple of crushed garlic cloves for the rosemary.

SERVES 4, PREP 3 MINS (PLUS MARINATING TIME)

225 g / 8 oz large juicy black olives
225 g / 8 oz large juicy green olives
4 rosemary sprigs

200 g / 7 oz Feta cheese, diced
150 ml / 5 fl oz olive oil

Mix everything together and leave to marinate. Take to work in little pots or serve as part of lunch.

TZATZIKI WITH CRUDITÉS

Every now and then it's nice to have a pot of something to dip crisps or vegetables into. If you are one of those people who find that by 11 o'clock your tummy is rumbling and you need a snack, this might be just what you need to see you through to lunch. It's a healthy snack, so you don't need to feel guilty about eating it.

SERVES 4, PREP 15 MINS (PLUS CHILLING TIME)

1 tbsp olive oil
1 tbsp white wine vinegar
225 g / 8 oz Greek yoghurt
sea salt flakes and ground black pepper
1 cucumber

a handful of fresh mint, chopped
a handful of fresh dill, chopped
crisps or vegetable matchsticks of your choice, for dipping

Whisk together the olive oil, vinegar and yoghurt in a bowl. Season to taste. Peel the cucumber, halve it lengthways, scoop out the seeds and dice the flesh. Add the cucumber, mint and dill to the yoghurt mixture. Chill, then serve with crisps or lots of fresh vegetable matchsticks.

CHICKEN GOUJONS WITH DIPPING SAUCE

I'm not going to keep saying it, but please remember to keep the chicken in the fridge until you are ready to eat. Little goujons are great hot or cold. I have included recipes like this in the book so that if you find yourself at home for lunch you can heat them quickly in the oven. They are also delicious for eating in front of the television.

SERVES 4, PREP 15 MINS (PLUS 20 MINS CHILLING TIME), COOKING 15 MINS

FOR THE GOUJONS
2 eggs
1 tbsp oil
sea salt flakes and ground black pepper
4 chicken breasts, cut into strips
125 g / 4 oz plain flour
225 g / 8 oz brown breadcrumbs
oil, for deep-frying

FOR THE DIPPING SAUCE
5 tbsp soy sauce
2 tbsp sesame oil
1/2 tsp caster sugar
1 1/2 tbsp white wine vinegar
1 tbsp peeled and finely diced fresh root ginger
1 spring onion, finely sliced

Whisk together the eggs and measured oil. Season the chicken strips well, then dip them in the flour one at a time. Shake off any excess, then dip in the beaten egg and shake off the excess. Place in the crumbs and coat, gently patting them in place. Cover with greaseproof paper and refrigerate for at least 20 minutes so the crumbs will set.

Mix together all the dipping sauce ingredients, then chill. Heat half a pan of oil until really hot, then fry the chicken pieces for 5 minutes or until cooked. Drain on kitchen paper and serve with the dipping sauce.

CAJUN STICKY CHICKEN WINGS

These are slightly hot, sticky and delicious. You don't need to add oil to the pan as the chicken creates its own oils and juices during cooking. They are just scrumptious taken to work in a pot for lunch with some crisp fresh watercress to accompany.

MAKES 15, PREP 10 MINS, COOKING 25 MINS

1 tsp coriander seeds
1 tsp cardamom seeds
zest of $1/2$ lemon
2 tsp paprika
2 tsp dried red chilli flakes

1 tbsp mixed spice
2 tbsp golden syrup
5 tbsp tomato sauce
15 chicken wings

Preheat the oven to 200 °C / 400 °F / gas mark 6. Dry-fry the coriander and cardamom seeds for a few minutes until golden. Crush with a pestle and mortar. Transfer to a bowl and add all the remaining ingredients except the chicken wings. Mix together well. Pluck any remaining feathers from the chicken and dry the wings on kitchen paper. Coat the chicken wings with the spice mixture using a pastry brush. Lay the chicken straight on to a heavy-based ovenproof dish (preferably non-stick) and bake for 10 minutes. Turn the wings over, baste with the juices and cook for another 10 minutes. Turn the wings once again, baste with the juices and cook for another 5 minutes.

SAFFRON AND HONEY PRAWNS

Saffron – the single most expensive spice. More than a quarter of a million crocus flowers must be harvested and the three stigmas from each crocus collected by hand to obtain 450 g / 1 lb of saffron. Fortunately very little is needed in cooking to add a delicate flavour and wonderful brilliant yellow colour. Soaking or grinding the threads before use brings out the strongest colour and flavour. It has a wonderful affinity with fish, garlic, poultry, beef and sweetbreads.

SERVES 4, PREP 10 MINS, COOKING 3 MINS

2 tbsp clear honey
juice of 2 lemons
1 large chilli, seeded and finely chopped
4 tbsp olive oil

a large pinch of saffron
2 garlic cloves, peeled and finely chopped
450 g / 1 lb uncooked prawns
sea salt flakes and ground black pepper

Mix together the honey, lemon juice, chilli, oil, saffron and garlic in a bowl. Shell the prawns, leave the tails on, add to the bowl of marinade ingredients and mix to coat. Heat a wok or frying pan, add the prawns and cook for about 3 minutes until firm. Season to taste with sea salt and ground black pepper.

HONEY SOY PRAWNS AND SCALLOPS WITH CUCUMBER SALSA

This recipe may appear slightly sophisticated for lunch, but we are not always looking for food to grab and eat. Sometimes you need to treat yourself.

SERVES 4, PREP 5 MINS, COOKING 25–30 MINS

1 small red chilli, seeded and finely chopped
2.5 cm / 1 in piece of root ginger, peeled and finely chopped
2 garlic cloves, peeled and crushed
4 tbsp runny honey
2 tbsp soy sauce

450 g / 1 lb large fresh prawns, peeled and trimmed
450 g / 1 lb fresh scallops, trimmed
1/2 cucumber
1 tsp caster sugar
2 tbsp rice wine vinegar
2 lemons, cut into wedges

Soak four wooden skewers in water. Place the chilli, ginger and garlic in a bowl. Add the honey and soy sauce and mix together well. Put the prawns and scallops into the marinade and coat each piece thoroughly. Heat a griddle pan until really hot. Thread the fish on to the skewers and grill for 5–10 minutes until the prawns and scallops are cooked through.

Meanwhile, halve the cucumber, scoop out and discard the seeds with a teaspoon and slice into thin strips with a vegetable peeler. Spoon the cucumber into a bowl. Mix together the sugar and vinegar and drizzle over the cucumber. When the skewers of prawns and scallops are cool, wrap up in foil or put into a container. Serve with lemon wedges and a fork for the cucumber salsa.

CHILLI PRAWNS WITH LIME AND SAFFRON SERVED WITH GARLIC MAYONNAISE

These are scrumptious dipped into the garlic mayonnaise and nibbled. Just take a pot of the prawns and a separate pot of mayonnaise and away you go (the usual rule applies – keep in the fridge until you are ready to eat). Alternatively, they make a wonderful sandwich filling: choose a couple of slices of soft bread, spread each with a little garlic mayonnaise and sandwich the prawns inside. They're such versatile little things.

SERVES 4, PREP 10 MINS (PLUS 30 MINS CHILLING TIME), COOKING 6 MINS

8 tbsp mayonnaise
3 garlic cloves, peeled and crushed
juice of 1 lime
20 raw headless prawns, thawed if frozen

a pinch of sea salt flakes
1 tsp chilli flakes
a pinch of saffron threads
2-3 tbsp vegetable oil
a handful of coriander leaves, chopped

Mix together the mayonnaise, half the garlic and half the lime juice. Put to one side. Peel the prawns, keeping the tails on. Put in a bowl, sprinkle with the salt, add the rest of the garlic, the chilli, saffron and remaining lime juice. Chill for at least 30 minutes. Heat the oil in a small frying pan. Add half the prawns and cook for 2–3 minutes, turning once, until they are pink. Drain on kitchen paper, then transfer to a bowl. Repeat with the remaining prawns. Add the coriander leaves and toss everything together.

MARINATED SCALLOPS WRAPPED IN BACON

These had to be included. Hot or cold, they're yummy.

MAKES 15, PREP 10 MINS, COOKING 10–12 MINS

15 scallops
5 cm / 2 in piece of fresh root ginger,
peeled and grated
3 tbsp soy sauce or Worcestershire
sauce

1 garlic clove, peeled and crushed
15 rashers bacon
oil, for brushing

Preheat the oven to 200 °C / 400 °F / gas mark 6. If the scallops are huge, halve them widthways (if you do this you will need more bacon). Place in a bowl. Mix together the ginger, soy or Worcestershire sauce and garlic, pour over the scallops and leave to marinate for 30 minutes. Halve the bacon lengthways and stretch each piece using the back of a knife. Wrap a bacon strip around a scallop, then wrap a second around the first to enclose the scallop. Put on a baking sheet and repeat with the remaining scallops and bacon. Brush with oil and bake for 10–12 minutes until crisp.

SPICY MUSHROOMS

It's so easy to make up dishes like these and just keep them in the fridge for a couple of days.

SERVES 4, PREP 10 MINS (PLUS 1 HOUR MARINATING TIME)

65 ml / 2 1/2 fl oz olive oil
450 g / 1 lb button mushrooms
1 tsp paprika

50 ml / 2 fl oz balsamic vinegar
2 garlic cloves, peeled and crushed
sea salt flakes and ground black pepper

Mix together all the ingredients together in a bowl, seasoning to taste. Leave to marinate for at least 1 hour before serving.

PARMESAN COURGETTES

This is a bit like the spicy mushroom recipe, and it keeps just as well in the fridge. Make up few for a nibble to go with drinks and take the rest for lunch.

SERVES 4, PREP 10 MINS, COOKING 20 MINS

4 courgettes
6 slices of white bread
125 g / 4 oz pine nuts, crushed

50 g / 2 oz Parmesan cheese, grated
25 g / 1 oz parsley, roughly chopped
sea salt flakes and ground black pepper

Preheat the oven to 200 °C / 400 °F / gas mark 6. Halve the courgettes lengthways, scoop out the seeds and discard. Crumb the bread into a bowl, add the pine nuts, Parmesan and parsley. Mix together and spoon into the courgettes. Season well and cook for 20 minutes. Serve hot or cold.

CHÈVRE WITH HERBS

If you are not a big fan of goat's cheese (chèvre) use cream cheese instead. If you fancy a lower-fat version, use low-fat cream cheese and loosen the mixture with a little yoghurt instead of double cream.

SERVES 4, PREP 10 MINS

300 g / 11 oz chèvre
1 tbsp double cream
50 g / 2 oz flat leaf parsley, roughly chopped

vegetable matchsticks or crisps, for dipping

Mix together the chèvre, cream and parsley in a bowl. Serve with vegetable matchsticks or crisps.

CHERRY TOMATOES, MOZZARELLA
AND FRESH BASIL KEBABS

Sometimes, developing a new recipe idea is all about creating a different way of serving a classic combination. This recipe is based on the popular salad of tomatoes, Mozzarella cheese and fresh basil. Buffalo Mozzarella is best, and make sure the tomatoes are really ripe.

SERVES 4, PREP 15 MINS

200 g / 7 oz Mozzarella cheese, cubed
225 g / 8 oz ripe cherry tomatoes
a couple of large handfuls of fresh basil leaves

3 tbsp extra virgin olive oil
sea salt flakes and ground black pepper

Thread the Mozzarella on to small sticks alternately with the tomatoes and some of the basil leaves. Place in a bowl or container. Drizzle over the oil, season to taste and scatter more basil leaves over the top.

SAUSAGES WITH SOY AND MARMALADE

I have lost count of the times I have made soy sausages of one kind or another. They are so easy and always popular, so take a pot to lunch with a little bag of fresh watercress to nibble on and the only problem you will have will be keeping your friends or colleagues away!

SERVES 4, PREP 10 MINS, COOKING 25–30 MINS

4 tbsp marmalade
3 tbsp soy sauce
2 tbsp white wine vinegar
1 tsp Chinese five spice powder

2 garlic cloves, peeled and crushed
30 cocktail sausages
fresh rocket or watercress, to serve

Preheat the oven to 220 °C / 425 °F / gas mark 7. In a bowl, mix together the marmalade, soy sauce, vinegar, five spice powder and garlic. Transfer to a small roasting pan, add the sausages and toss to coat. Bake the sausages for about 25–30 minutes, turning occasionally, until nicely browned.

MASALA SAMOSAS

Great with drinks in the evening, brilliant warm or cold for lunch. If you want to reduce the preparation time, use a bought garam masala.

SERVES 4, PREP 20–30 MINS, COOKING 25–30 MINS

FOR THE GARAM MASALA
4 tbsp coriander seeds
2 tbsp cumin seeds
1 tsp peppercorns
1 tsp cardamom seeds from the pod
1 long cinnamon stick, broken in half
1 tsp whole cloves
1 whole nutmeg

FOR THE TIKKA PASTE
1 tsp garam masala (see above)
1 tsp dried ginger
1 tsp ground cumin
1 tsp turmeric
2 tsp paprika
1/2 tsp dried chilli powder
5 tbsp water
3 tbsp sunflower oil
2–3 garlic cloves, peeled and crushed
to a smooth paste
1 tsp tamarind paste

1/2 large chilli, finely chopped
1 oz coriander leaves, finely chopped

FOR THE SAMOSA FILLING
225 g / 8 oz chickpeas, soaked
overnight
410 g / 14 1/2 oz can of chickpeas
125 g / 4 oz fresh green peas, cooked
2 tbsp tikka paste (see above)
1 large red onion, peeled and sliced
juice of 1 lime
25 g / 1 oz coriander leaves, chopped
sea salt flakes
ground black pepper
12–15 sheets frozen filo pastry,
defrosted
sunflower oil, for greasing OR for
deep-frying
6 tbsp natural Greek yoghurt
whole coriander leaves, to serve

To prepare the garam masala, roast the coriander and cumin seeds, peppercorns, cardamom, cinnamon sticks and cloves separately until each spice releases its fragrance. (Roasting brings out the flavour and makes grinding them easier.) Blend together in a food processor or with a pestle and mortar. Grate in the nutmeg and mix. Store in an airtight jar.

To make the tikka paste, mix together all the spices. Add the water, then the oil, and blend together thoroughly. Add the garlic, tamarind, chilli and coriander. Mix well and set aside in a covered bowl or jar with a lid.

To make the samosa filling, drain the soaked chick peas, place in a food processor and purée for about 15 seconds until smooth. Roughly mash with a fork the canned chick peas and half the liquid from the can, leaving just a few chick peas nearly whole. Mix with the chick pea purée. Add the green peas, tikka paste, onion, lime juice and chopped coriander and season to taste with salt and ground black pepper.

To assemble the samosas, take a sheet of filo pastry, fold it in half lengthways and place 2–3 tbsp of the chick pea mixture at one end. Fold over one corner to make a triangle. Continue folding this way to make a triangular package, sealing the edges with water. Repeat with the remaining pastry and filling.

To cook, preheat the oven to 180 °C / 350 °F / gas mark 4. Place the samosas on a greased baking tray, brush with a little oil and bake in the oven for 25–30 minutes until golden. Alternatively, deep-fry a few at a time in sunflower oil until golden brown all over. Drain on kitchen paper. Mix together the remaining tikka paste and the yoghurt. Serve with the samosas, garnished with coriander leaves.

WARM SUN-DRIED TOMATO AND HERB SCONES

Hot scones straight from the oven served dipped in olive oil with a chunk of Parmesan cheese. Or leave to cool and then freeze. There are endless variations you can try, perhaps swap the tomatoes for cheese and herbs.

MAKES 10, PREP 15 MINS, COOKING 15 MINS

200 g / 7 oz self-raising flour
1/2 tsp baking powder
1/2 tsp sea salt flakes
50 g / 2 oz sun-dried tomatoes, roughly chopped
25 g / 1 oz fresh parsley, roughly chopped

4 tbsp extra virgin olive oil
1 medium egg
75 ml / 3 fl oz milk
25 g / 1 oz Parmesan cheese, grated
extra olive oil and Parmesan cheese, to serve

Preheat the oven to 220 °C / 425 °F / gas mark 7. Sift the flour, baking powder and salt into a bowl. Stir in the tomatoes and parsley. Make a well in the centre. Mix together the oil, egg and milk and pour into the well. Blend everything together but do not beat. Drop 10 little spoonfuls on to a baking sheet, sprinkle with the grated cheese and bake for 12–14 minutes until golden brown and cooked through. Eat warm with olive oil for dipping and a chunk of Parmesan cheese.

CRISPY CHEESE BISCUITS

These can be eaten as soon as they come out of the oven, or taken to work for lunch, or frozen. They are great for children to make and they are also delicious served hot and crispy with drinks for adults.

MAKES APPROX 12, PREP 15 MINS, COOKING 8–12 MINS

125 g / 4 oz Cheddar cheese, grated
50 g / 2 oz butter, softened
65 g / 2¹/₂ oz plain flour, sieved

¹/₄ tsp sea salt flakes
cayenne pepper
25 g / 1 oz crisped rice cereal

Preheat the oven to 190 °C / 375 °F / gas mark 5. Combine the cheese, butter, flour and salt and add cayenne to taste. Crush the cereal with a rolling pin, add to the cheese mixture and mix everything together. Mould the mixture into tiny balls (about 5 ml / 1 tsp each), arrange on a baking sheet and flatten with a fork. Bake for 8–12 minutes (they don't take long, so check them after 8 minutes).

SOUPS

Chunky, smooth, hot or cold – however they come and whatever the weather, soups are perfect for lunchboxes.

Smooth hot soups like creamy tomato are delicious in a mug with a sandwich alongside; chunky soups such as leek, potato and bacon are so filling they are a meal in themselves; and light soups can be perfect with a hunk of bread or a salad. A thermos flask of chilled soup taken to work can make a refreshing summer lunch.

Anyone who can cut up a vegetable can whiz up one of these soups in only a little more time than it takes to open a tin. Most soups improve in flavour over a day or so, so if you make the soup for dinner and keep a portion for lunch the next day it will be really delicious. They also freeze brilliantly. With a couple of frozen soups on standby anguished mornings wondering what on earth to have for lunch will be a thing of the past.

The individual character of all dishes comes from the life and experience of the cook, and somehow this seems particularly the case when it comes to soup. You should find soups that you enjoy making and eating. Choose different ones depending on the ingredients you have to hand, your mood and the setting.

As with all recipes, the key to success in your soups is largely dependent on the quality of the ingredients used. A fundamental example of this is the stock, the base to your soups. If I have not made a stock, I will use good quality bouillon powders, but never a stock cube. To me the flavour of cubes overpowers the rest of the soup. Likewise, if you begin with poor quality vegetables, how do you expect to end up with a delicious vegetable soup? I do feel that blenders give the best result when you are making a smooth soup, compared with food processors or hand-held blenders. Texture can be very important and if you're expecting a soup to be really smooth and what you get is bitty or grainy it can really ruin the overall enjoyment of the dish. It's also worth investing in one of the really excellent thermos flasks available nowadays.

I often take a pot of 'little bits' like bacon, croûtons, chopped egg and tomatoes to scatter over the top just before eating soup (which are also great for nibbling on mid-morning, if you get really peckish!). Also, often, just by adding a spoon of pesto or a handful of roasted nuts, soups that may otherwise at first glance appear quite plain, become interesting and packed with flavour and texture.

I have really enjoyed creating the recipes for this section, which I have sorted into smooth, chunky, chilled and hot soups. Now you just need to have fun making them and if you want to change the spices, herbs or other flavour combinations, go right ahead.

CHILLED SOUPS

Most of these soups can be frozen, either pour into plastic containers or freeze in portion sizes in small bags so that they are easy to defrost.

TOMATO AND BASIL

I do not need to say very much about this soup, it speaks for itself. The only point I will make is that you really need to use ripe tomatoes that have a lot of flavour. If the tomatoes are bland, the soup will be bland.

SERVES 4, PREP 15 MINS, COOKING 5 MINS

25 g / 1 oz butter
1 medium onion, peeled and finely sliced
1 garlic clove, peeled and finely chopped
1 stick celery, finely chopped

1 kg / 2.2 lbs ripe tomatoes, chopped
568 ml / 1 pint vegetable stock
1 tsp lemon juice
1 tsp brown sugar
sea salt flakes and ground black pepper
a handful of fresh basil

Heat the butter in a large saucepan; add the onion, garlic and celery, cook gently until soft, not brown. Add the tomatoes, the stock and half of the basil. Bring quickly to the boil and simmer for 5 minutes. Blend the soup in batches until smooth, then pass through a sieve pushing the liquid through with a spoon. Cool and refrigerate for 1 1/2 hours. Add the lemon juice and sugar to taste. Roughly tear the basil leaves and scatter over the soup, stir gently to combine.

BEETROOT

The key to successful beetroot soup is to use fresh beetroot and purée it with the cooking liquid because the beetroot leaches its colour, flavour and goodness as it cooks. So it is vital that the cooking liquid is included in the soup rather than being thrown away.

SERVES 4, PREP 15 MINS, COOKING 50 MINS

25 g / 1 oz butter
1 onion, finely chopped
1 medium sized potato, peeled and cubed
700 g / 1 1/2 lb beetroot, peeled and cubed
900 ml / 1 1/2 pints chicken or vegetable stock

2 tbsp red wine vinegar
300 ml / 1/2 pint sour cream
sea salt flakes and ground black pepper
juice of 1 lemon
fresh chives, to serve

Melt the butter in a saucepan and cook the onion until golden brown. Add the potato and beetroot and cook, stirring constantly for one minute. Add the stock and vinegar. Bring to the boil, cover and simmer gently for 45 minutes.

Take the soup from the heat and leave to cool. Purée in a blender (or food processor) until really smooth. If necessary thin it down with a little extra stock. Add the cream and blend again. Season to taste, adding a little lemon juice if necessary. Scatter over some fresh chives, finely chopped.

SPICY GAZPACHO

Soups do not get simpler than this – even my husband made it! He loved it, and then asked me why it took so long to develop the recipes for this book when they are so easy! There are two really cool ways to enjoy this soup, either served with crunchy croûtons or a big bunch of fresh, wild rocket leaves on top.

SERVES 4, PREP 20 MINS

900 g / 2 lb very ripe cherry tomatoes or baby plum tomatoes, roughly chopped
1 cucumber, peeled, seeded and chopped
1 clove garlic, peeled and chopped
1 red chilli, seeded and finely chopped

2 spring onions, finely chopped
4 tbsp extra virgin olive oil
1 tbsp red wine vinegar
1 tbsp golden caster sugar
sea salt flakes and ground black pepper
cayenne pepper

Put all of the ingredients, except seasoning, into a food processor. Whiz until smooth. Season to taste with sea salt flakes, ground black pepper and cayenne pepper.

LEEK, FENNEL AND LEMON

This is a really refreshing, subtly flavoured soup, and the lemon gives the whole dish a little kick. Fennel has an aniseed flavour that becomes slightly more intense with the addition of the tarragon. Obviously, this soup is great for a lunch but it is also delicious served as starter as it provokes and entices the palate ready to enjoy the rest of the meal.

SERVES 4, PREP 15 MINS, COOKING 35 MINS

450 g / 1 lb leeks, finely sliced
1 large fennel bulb
1 small onion, peeled and sliced
1.1 litres / 2 pints vegetable stock

2 tbsp of chopped fresh tarragon
sea salt flakes and ground black pepper
300 ml / 1/2 pint single cream
juice of 1 lemon

Halve the fennel lengthways and slice into thin strips. Melt the butter in a saucepan. Add the onion, leeks and fennel and cook over a gentle heat, stirring frequently, until just turning translucent and brown at the edges. Add the stock, half the tarragon and a pinch of salt, bring to the boil and simmer gently for approximately 30 minutes until the fennel is soft. Allow to cool, then blend the soup in a food processor until really smooth. Stir in the cream and remaining tarragon. Add the lemon juice and season to taste.

CUCUMBER, MINT AND YOGHURT

This literally takes about 20 minutes to make without turning the oven on. Just remember to allow 2 hours for chilling.

SERVES 6, PREP 20 MINS

1 large cucumber
1 tbsp sea salt flakes
450 ml / 15 fl oz / ¾ pint pot natural yoghurt
2 cloves garlic, peeled and finely chopped

568 ml / 1 pint vegetable stock
50 g / 2 oz fresh mint, washed and roughly chopped
a handful of mint leaves and lemon juice, to serve

Halve the cucumber lengthways and scoop out the seeds. Finely chop one third of the flesh and leave to one side. Peel and finely chop the remaining cucumber, sprinkle with salt and leave to drain for 30 minutes. Rinse and squeeze out any excess moisture on to kitchen paper. Blend together the yoghurt, garlic and vegetable stock in a food processor or blender. Add the drained cucumber and blend until smooth. Add the chopped mint. Season and add lemon juice to taste. Chill for at least 2 hours. Scatter the reserved cucumber over the top and serve garnished with mint leaves and lemon juice to taste.

SUMMER FRUITS WITH APPLE

This could be a light lunch, breakfast, pudding or starter. If you do want to serve it as a pudding, add scoops of sorbet or ice cream to the middle and, for a real flourish, pour sparkling wine over the top. Watch the guests' faces as the sorbet bubbles and fizzes. Star anise is a star-shaped spice with an aniseed flavour and a pronounced element of liquorice.

SERVES 4, PREP 15 MINS, COOKING 15 MINS

200 ml / 7 fl oz fresh pineapple juice
100 ml / 3½ fl oz smoothie (buy a good smoothie or make your own using a handful of fresh strawberries, juice of 1 orange and a banana; whiz in a food processor until smooth)
100 ml / 3½ fl oz freshly squeezed orange juice

juice of ½ lime
2 apples, peeled, cored and chopped into bite-sized pieces
1 star anise pod
350 g / 12 oz assorted berries (raspberries, blueberries, strawberries)
a handful of fresh, tiny, mint leaves, roughly torn

Put the pineapple juice, smoothie, orange juice, apple and star anise in a saucepan. Bring up to the boil and gently simmer for about 15 minutes or until the apple is tender. Transfer to a large bowl to cool. Remove the star anise and stir through the lime juice, berries and mint leaves.

HOT SOUPS – SMOOTH

BUTTER BEAN WITH FRESH PARSLEY

There are so many types of canned beans and chick peas available that I very rarely use the dried variety nowadays.

SERVES 6, PREP 10 MINS, COOKING 10 MINS

2 tbsp olive oil
2 cloves garlic, peeled and finely chopped
a handful of fresh flat leaf parsley
900 ml / 1 1/2 pints vegetable stock

2 x 400 g / 14 oz cans butter beans
sea salt flakes and ground black pepper
50 g / 2 oz fresh Parmesan
extra virgin olive oil, to serve

Heat the oil in a frying pan, add the garlic and half of the parsley and cook very gently without browning. Add the stock and beans, bring to the boil and simmer for 5 minutes. Transfer the beans in batches to a blender and purée until smooth. Return the beans to the saucepan, add the parsley and season to taste. Grate the cheese into large shavings and stir into the soup with olive oil to taste.

SWEET POTATO AND WALNUT

Orange-fleshed sweet potatoes, the tropical root vegetable, have the most amazing colour and flavour and are a delightful soup ingredient. You just have to be careful not to overcook them. You will see that I don't use flour to thicken any of my soups: I would far rather use vegetables like potatoes, bread and pasta. In this recipe the potatoes give the soup its smooth and creamy texture.

SERVES 4, PREP 15 MINS, COOKING 25 MINS

25 g / 1 oz butter
1 large onion, peeled and finely chopped
700 g / 1 1/2 lb sweet potatoes, peeled and finely chopped
900 ml / 1 1/2 pints vegetable stock
50 g / 2 oz walnuts, toasted and chopped

sea salt flakes and ground black pepper
a handful of fresh flat leaf parsley, roughly chopped
2 rashers of streaky bacon, grilled and chopped (if you fancy)

Melt the butter in a large saucepan and fry the onion until golden brown. Add the potatoes and cook over a gentle heat for 5 minutes, stirring often. Add the stock and bring to the boil. Cover and simmer for 20–25 minutes or until the potatoes are soft. Add the walnuts. Allow to cool slightly, then purée in batches. Return to a clean pan, season to taste and stir through the parsley. Scatter crispy bacon over the top if you wish.

MUSHROOM AND CHESTNUT

You could add a few tablespoons of Marsala or sherry at the end of the
mushrooms' cooking time to make this soup perfect for a dinner party
– or to give it a bit of a kick on a cold winter day.

SERVES 4, PREP 15 MINS, COOKING 45 MINS

25 g / 1 oz butter
1 large onion, finely chopped
2 cloves garlic, crushed
900 g / 2 lbs open capped mushrooms
175 g / 6 oz unsweetened chestnut
purée

1/2 tsp grated nutmeg
sea salt flakes and ground black pepper
2 tbsp finely chopped parsley

Melt the butter in a saucepan, add the onion and garlic and fry until golden
brown. Add the mushrooms and cook for 5 minutes until they are just beginning
to lose their juice. Add the chestnut purée and nutmeg and a little salt and
pepper. Stir well and add the stock. Cover and simmer gently for 40 minutes.
Allow to cool slightly, then liquidise in batches and return to a clean saucepan.
Season to taste and stir in the parsley.

CREAMY TOMATO

This is good old-fashioned comfort food. You'll need to get the reddest, ripest most fragrant tomatoes you can find. Rock-hard greenhouse tomatoes just won't do! I have found no better way than roasting the tomatoes to really intensify their flavour – and while they are roasting, you can go and do something else!

SERVES 4, PREP 15 MINS, COOKING 45 MINS

25 g / 1 oz butter
1 small onion, peeled and finely chopped
1 clove of garlic, peeled
900 g / 2 lbs ripe tomatoes, roughly chopped

1 bay leaf
a handful each of fresh thyme and parsley
sea salt flakes and ground black pepper
1.1 litre / 2 pts vegetable stock
200 ml / 7 fl oz double cream

Preheat the oven to 200 °C / 400 °F/ gas mark 6. Put the butter in a large roasting tin and melt it on the hob. Add the onion, garlic, tomatoes, bay leaf, thyme and parsley to the pan, season and mix everything together. Cook for a couple of minutes, then remove from the heat, cover with foil and roast for 40 minutes, stirring once during cooking. Remove the bay leaf and herbs from the pan. Liquidise the tomatoes in batches in a food processor with some of the stock. Pass the soup through a sieve into a clean saucepan to remove all the pips and skin. Add the rest of the stock and the cream. Reheat gently, adjusting the seasoning to taste.

ROASTED PEPPER

Roasting vegetables intensifies their flavour and concentrates their natural sweetness. In this recipe, you throw everything in the oven and leave it to cook, then whiz it in a food processor with vegetable stock. Couldn't be easier. If you don't have any fresh vegetable stock, use bouillon powder rather than stock cubes.

SERVES 4, PREP 15 MINS, COOKING 50 MINS

1 red onion, peeled and chopped
2 cloves garlic, peeled
1 carrot, washed and roughly chopped
1 celery stick, sliced
1 leek, washed and thickly sliced
2 yellow peppers, seeded and roughly chopped
3 red peppers, seeded and roughly chopped

1 fresh mild red chilli, seeded and chopped
1 tbsp olive oil
pinch saffron threads
sea salt flakes and ground black pepper
900 ml / 1 1/2 pint vegetable stock

Preheat the oven to 200 °C / 400 °F / gas mark 6. Put all of the vegetables in an ovenproof dish; add the chilli, oil and the saffron and season well. Roast for 45 minutes or until the peppers are soft and cooked. Transfer to a food processor; add half of the stock and whiz until smooth. Sieve into a saucepan. Add enough of the remaining stock to make the consistency you want. Adjust the seasoning, heat through and serve.

WATERCRESS

This is really delicious with crusty bread and a chunk of Roquefort cheese.

SERVES 4, PREP 15 MINS, COOKING 30 MINS

25 g / 1 oz butter
1 tbsp olive oil
4 shallots, peeled and finely chopped
1 celery stalk, trimmed and finely chopped
1 small carrot, peeled and finely chopped

500 g / 1 1/4 lb peeled and diced potatoes
1.1 litres / 2 pints vegetable stock
sea salt flakes and ground black pepper
3 bunches of watercress, well washed and stalks taken off
150 ml / 5 fl oz double cream

Melt the butter and oil in a large saucepan. Add the shallots, celery and carrot, sauté over a medium heat until they are soft and just golden brown. Add the potatoes and cook 2 minutes, stirring constantly. Add the stock and a pinch of salt. Bring to the boil, then simmer for 20 minutes, or until the potatoes are soft. Add the watercress and cook for five minutes longer. Liquidise in a food processor until smooth. Return to the saucepan. Add the cream and season before gently reheating.

CURRIED PARSNIP

This is also really nice with roughly chopped toasted cashew nuts mixed with a little sea salt sprinkled over the top.

SERVES 4, PREP 20 MINS, COOKING 30 MINS

40 g / 1½ oz butter
1 large onion, peeled and finely chopped
2 garlic cloves, peeled and crushed
700 g / 1½ lbs parsnips, peeled and chopped
225 g / 8 oz potatoes, peeled and chopped

1 dtsp curry powder
2 litres / 3½ pints of chicken or vegetable stock
sea salt flakes and ground black pepper
200 ml / 7 fl oz single cream
a handful of fresh parsley, roughly chopped

Melt the butter in a large heavy-based saucepan; add the onion, garlic, parsnips and potatoes. Cover the pan and cook gently for 15 minutes – keep an eye on it and stir a couple of times to prevent sticking. Add the curry powder and cook for two minutes, stirring constantly. Add the stock and bring to the boil, still stirring, then simmer for about 10–15 minutes until the parsnips and potatoes are soft. Transfer to a blender, season to taste and purée until really smooth. Reheat and add the cream and parsley.

QUICK COURGETTE

This is delicious with warm baguettes – or try part-baked garlic bread available from many supermarkets. I've made this recipe lots of times and no-one's ever guessed the secret ingredient!

SERVES 4, PREP 10 MINS, COOKING 10 MINS

6 medium sized courgettes
1.1 litres / 2 pints vegetable stock
1 packet cheese spread triangles

sea salt flakes and ground black pepper
a handful of fresh parsley, roughly chopped

Wash and roughly chop the courgettes. Bring the stock to the boil in a pan, add the courgettes and boil quickly for about 5–8 minutes until tender. Remove from the heat and add the cheese triangles. Using a hand blender or food processor whiz until smooth. Season to taste and add the parsley.

ZINGY CITRUS CARROT

I try to cook vegetables for the minimum time they need. This way, not only are you more likely to benefit from their nutritional value, but their flavour will also be at its best. This soup is a fine example of how lightly cooked vegetables like carrots can very easily make a delicious soup.

SERVES 4, PREP 15 MINS, COOKING 10–15 MINS

25 g / 1 oz butter
1 large onion, peeled and finely chopped
1.1 kg / 2½ lbs carrots, peeled and grated
1.1 litre / 2 pints vegetable stock

juice of 1 large orange
juice of 1 lemon
sea salt flakes and ground black pepper
a handful of flat leaf parsley, roughly chopped

Melt the butter in a large saucepan, add the onion and cook until soft and just turning golden. Add the carrots and cook, stirring constantly for 5 minutes. Pour over the stock, bring to the boil and simmer for 5–10 minutes until the carrots are just tender. Purée with a hand blender or in a food processor. Add the orange and lemon juice. Season to taste and stir through the parsley.

HOT CHUNKY SOUPS

THAI ROASTED SWEETCORN AND COCONUT CHOWDER

So filling it is definitely a complete meal on its own; it is bursting with flavour.

SERVES 4, PREP 20 MINS, COOKING 30 MINS

6 ears fresh corn or 500 g / 1 1/4 lbs canned sweetcorn
1 large onion, peeled and finely chopped
3 cloves garlic, peeled and crushed
2.5 cm / 1 in piece of fresh root ginger, peeled and finely chopped
1 red chilli, halved and seeded and finely chopped

1 stick lemon grass, outer leaves removed
1 large potato, peeled and cut into small chunks
2 tbsp butter
400 ml tin coconut milk
325 ml / 11 fl oz vegetable stock
4 tbsp roughly chopped fresh coriander
juice of half a lime

Preheat oven 220 °C / 450 °F / gas mark 8. If using fresh corn cobs, peel away and discard the husks from each ear and place in a roasting pan with the onion, garlic cloves, ginger, chilli, lemon grass and potato. Mix together thoroughly. Dot the vegetables with the butter and roast for 30 minutes, then leave to cool. If using canned sweetcorn, roast all the other vegetables for 20 minutes, then add the corn and continue roasting for 10 minutes. Remove the lemon grass from the pan and discard. Scrape the kernels away from the cobs. Put the coconut milk and stock in a large saucepan; add the roasted corn and vegetables. Bring to the boil and simmer gently for 5 minutes. Stir in the coriander and lime juice and season to taste.

RICE NOODLE AND PRAWNS

A soup for lunch when you only have 15 minutes. Prepare the ingredients before you go to work and cook it when you come home for lunch. The garlic, ginger, chilli and carrot must be finely chopped as the soup is not puréed.

SERVES 4, PREP 15 MINS, COOKING 15 MINS

2 tbsp olive oil
2 garlic cloves, peeled and sliced
2.5 cm /1 in root ginger, peeled and sliced
1/2 red pepper, seeded and finely sliced
1 green chilli, seeded and sliced
2 carrots, thinly sliced

120 g / 4 1/2 oz yellow oyster mushrooms, torn into pieces
250 ml / 8 fl oz boiling water
250 ml / 8 fl oz chicken stock
200 g / 7 oz rice noodles
250 g / 9 oz tiger prawns, cooked
2 stalks lemongrass, halved
sea salt flakes and ground black pepper

Heat the oil in a saucepan. Add the garlic, ginger, red pepper, chilli, carrots and mushrooms and soften for 2–3 minutes. Add the boiling water and chicken stock, bring to the boil and simmer for 5 minutes. Add the rice noodles and cook for 5 minutes.

Add the prawns. Bash the lemongrass with a rolling pin a couple of times to bruise it slightly then add to the soup. Season to taste and serve.

TUSCAN BEAN

This soup is semi-chunky, but still warrants a place in this section. Eat it with a chunk of Parmesan cheese and some fresh bread and you have a complete meal.

SERVES 4, PREP 10 MINS, COOKING 35 MINS

2 tbsp oil
1 onion, peeled and roughly chopped
3 garlic cloves, peeled and roughly chopped
4 large thyme sprigs

1 bay leaf
2 x 400 g / 14 oz cans cannellini beans
225 ml / 8 fl oz chicken stock
juice of 1 lemon
sea salt flakes and ground black pepper

Heat the oil in a heavy-based saucepan. Add the onion, garlic, thyme and bay leaf. Sauté for at least 20 minutes or until the liquid has evaporated and the onion has caramelized. Add the beans and chicken stock, then bring to the boil. Reduce the heat and simmer for 15 minutes.

Discard the thyme and bay leaf. Purée the soup, in batches in a liquidiser or hand blender until smooth. Stir in the lemon juice and season with salt and ground black pepper.

ITALIAN CHICK PEA

This is really delicious served with dollops of pesto, either deli-bought or homemade (see page 151).

SERVES 4, PREP 15 MINS, COOKING 50 MINS

4 ripe tomatoes
2 tbsp olive oil
2 onions, peeled and finely chopped
2 garlic cloves, peeled and finely chopped
1 leek, finely sliced
2 sprigs fresh rosemary
200 g / 7 oz canned chick peas (with liquid)

1.1 litres / 2 pints vegetable stock
1 courgette, diced
125 g / 4 oz peas
125 g / 4 oz French beans, halved
125 g / 4 oz shelled broad beans
2 tbsp freshly chopped parsley
sea salt flakes and ground black pepper

Immerse the tomatoes in a bowl of boiling water for 10 seconds, then remove with a slotted spoon and peel away the skins. Chop the tomato flesh. Heat the oil in a large saucepan, add the onion, garlic, leek and rosemary and fry gently for 10 minutes until softened, but not coloured. Add the chick peas with their liquid, the stock and tomatoes. Bring to the boil, cover and simmer for 30 minutes. Add the courgette, peas and both beans. Return to the boil and simmer for a further 10 minutes. Add the parsley and cook for 3–4 minutes. Season to taste and serve.

Black bean and smoky bacon

Remember to taste before adding salt as smoked bacon is quite salty.

Serves 4, Prep 10 mins, Cooking 25 mins

1 tbsp olive oil
1 large onion, peeled and finely chopped
2 large green peppers, seeded and finely chopped
2 cloves garlic, peeled and crushed
1 x 420 g / 15 oz can black eyed beans

1 litre / 1¾ pints vegetable stock
2 tbsp black bean stir fry sauce
10 smoked back bacon rashers
1 tbsp sherry vinegar
sea salt flakes and ground black pepper

Heat the oil in a large saucepan and add the onion. Cover and cook over a medium heat until the onion is soft and translucent but not browned. Stir in the chopped peppers and garlic and cook for a further few minutes until soft. Add the beans, stock and black bean sauce and bring to the boil. Reduce the heat, cover the pan and cook gently for 15 minutes.

Meanwhile, finely chop the bacon, discarding any rinds. Place in a large frying pan and cook over a medium heat until crisp and golden brown. Add the bacon to the soup, together with any bacon fat in the pan. Stir in the sherry vinegar, season to taste and serve.

CHICKEN AND HERB

I always think of my late mother when I make chicken soup. It was her remedy for any cold or flu and I must say it always worked (with a little TLC as well). This soup contains chunks of potato, celery and leeks, as well as the chicken. No matter how small or big the chunks, the soup is definitely not smooth.

SERVES 4, PREP 15 MINS, COOKING 30 MINS

2 chicken breasts, with no skin
2 tbsp olive oil
1 red onion, peeled and diced
2 cloves garlic, crushed
2 celery stalks, washed and very finely diced
1 leek, washed and thinly sliced (white part only)

250 g / 9 oz red skinned potatoes peeled and cut into 1cm dice
1.7 litres / 3 pints chicken or vegetable stock
1 sprig of rosemary
1 sprig tarragon
1 sprig thyme
flat leaf parsley, to serve

Cut the chicken into 1 cm / ½ in chunks. Heat the oil in a large heavy-based saucepan, add the onion, garlic, celery and leek and sauté until golden brown. Transfer to a plate. Add the chicken to the pan and fry quickly until it's golden. Add the potatoes and cook for 1 minute, stirring constantly – the potatoes should be coated in oil. Return the onion mixture to the pan with the herbs and the stock, bring to the boil. Simmer for 20 minutes until the chicken is cooked and the potato is soft. Discard the herbs. Season to taste. Roughly chop the parsley and sprinkle over the top.

REAL SANDWICHES

In my opinion, there are sandwiches and then there are *real* sandwiches. I am the first to admit that a couple of slices of white bread with cold meat and sage and onion stuffing can have its appeal – especially at one in the morning. However, while sandwiches and leftovers go hand-in-hand, I think the best sandwiches are well thought through and use a variety of fresh ingredients.

No sandwich is better than its bread so it is worth experimenting with different loaves and rolls. Try some of the nutty breads like walnut or muesli; they're delicious with cheeses and fruits like dates and bananas. Also, look out for sourdoughs, cholla, sun-dried tomato, scofa, cheddar and onion – just a few of the many worth investigating.

The focaccias – like herb, tomato, mushroom and garlic, garlic and herb, tomato and herb, and black olive – are just delicious on their own. Or if they're slightly stale and crispy, halve them widthways, cover with toppings like tomato paste and cheese, and grill until bubbling.

If you are in a hurry, sandwiches like avocado with yoghurt and lime are as fast as they come. If you had chicken last night, throw together chicken with saffron mayonnaise and pepper sandwiches. If you are looking for a sweet fix in a roll, chop up some dates and mix with cream cheese and toasted almonds.

I have included recipes for fillings and toppings such as guacamole or salsa so you can make your own. But if time is short, use shop-bought dips, pâté, spreads and other fillings and assemble the sandwiches in the same combinations I have used.

Wrap sandwiches in greaseproof paper, not cling film which makes them sweat. Sandwiches are best kept in the fridge until lunchtime but taste better if allowed to come to room temperature before eating.

In this section, you will find sixty-nine sandwich ideas, both traditional and innovative. Notice that I say ideas and not recipes; use your imagination and mix and match the suggested ingredients. The key to great sandwich making is improvisation.

AVOCADO WITH YOGHURT, LIME AND RED ONION

This combination works really well, especially in summer when you are looking for fresh and zingy flavours. It makes a particularly good sandwich when made with olive foccacia. If you want a bit more protein in the sandwich, add a few chunks of tuna or a couple of slices of fresh turkey.

SERVES 4, PREP 10 MINS

3 avocados
juice of 1/2 lime
85 ml / 3 fl oz mayonnaise
65 ml / 2 fl oz natural yoghurt

1/2 red onion, peeled and chopped
sea salt flakes and ground black pepper
8 slices fresh bread

Halve the avocados, remove their stones and scoop out the flesh into a bowl. Add the lime juice and mash together until smooth. Add the mayonnaise and yoghurt and beat until smooth. Season to taste. Spread on four bread slices, scatter the red onion over the top and cover each with another slice of bread. Halve and wrap or serve.

ALFALFA SPROUTS WITH SPICY TOMATO SALSA AND HUMUS

A herb or tomato bread would work really well with this sandwich. Alfalfa sprouts are available from most big supermarkets or health food shops.

SERVES 4, PREP 10 MINS

150 g / 5 oz humus (see page 140 or use bought)
8 slices bread
225 g /8 oz alfalfa sprouts or cress

1 tsp Tabasco or other chilli sauce
125 g /4 oz tomato salsa
(see page 154)

Spread the humus between four slices of the bread. Top with the alfalfa sprouts. Mix the chilli sauce into the salsa and spoon on top of the alfalfa sprouts. Cover each with another slice of bread. Halve and wrap or serve.

SPICY GUACAMOLE WITH ROASTED VEGETABLES

The pungent ingredients added to this guacomole really enhance the flavour of the avocado and its texture is a great contrast with the roasted vegetables. You really don't need any butter or mayo in this sandwich – it's perfect as it is. It would be delicious made with foccacia or a crusty baguette or ciabatta.

SERVES 4, PREP 20 MINS

2 cloves garlic, peeled and crushed
2 ripe avocados, peeled, halved and stoned
1 fresh red chilli, seeded and chopped
juice of 1/2 a lemon
2 plum tomatoes, finely chopped
1 spring onion, finely chopped

1 tsp Tabasco
sea salt flakes and ground black pepper
2 tbsp roughly chopped coriander
8 slices bread
selection of roasted vegetables (see page 139 or use bought ones)

Place the garlic and avocados in a bowl. Add the chilli, lemon juice, tomatoes, onion, Tabasco, salt, pepper and coriander. Mash together well until the mixture is as chunky or smooth as you like. Spread between all the slices of bread. Top four slices with the roasted vegetables and cover other four slices. Halve and wrap or serve.

GRILLED AUBERGINE, WITH GOAT'S CHEESE IN PITTA

Pitta bread is perfect for sandwiches – it's a natural container. If you're making this sandwich at lunchtime at home try toasting the pitta before adding the filling. It's delicious hot, especially on a chilly day.

SERVES 4, PREP 15 MINS, COOKING 15–20 MINS

1 large aubergine
3 tbsp extra virgin olive oil
225 g / 8 oz goat's cheese

1 bunch fresh basil leaves
4 pitta breads
sea salt flakes and ground black pepper

Trim off and discard the tops of the aubergine. Cut lengthways into thin strips. Brush with half of the oil and grill them in batches until golden, turning once. Mix the cheese with the basil and remaining oil. Season to taste. Slice open the pitta breads, line them with the grilled aubergine, stuff with the cheese mixture and season again if necessary.

AUBERGINE BUTTER WITH WALNUTS

This is incredibly satisfying and quite rich. It's best taken to work in a separate pot and eaten with some fresh bread rolls, or spread into a French stick and sprinkled with lots of fresh coriander. This recipe makes quite a lot but it keeps well in the fridge in a sealed jar. It's delicious on toast, in jacket potatoes, with cold lamb or with salads.

SERVES 4, PREP 20 MINS, COOKING 40 MINS (PLUS 30 MINS STANDING TIME)

1.1 kg / 2¹/₂ lb aubergines
2 tbsp olive oil
2 cloves garlic, peeled
2 tbsp sherry vinegar
juice of 1 lemon
150 g / 5 oz walnuts

salt salt and ground black pepper
50 ml / 5 fl oz extra virgin olive oil
1 fresh French stick, sliced
chopped coriander leaves (optional), to serve

Put the aubergines under a preheated hot grill for about 40 minutes, turning occasionally, until the skin is black and blistered all over (this gives the aubergines a smoky flavour). Peel off the skins, halve the aubergines lengthways and scoop out the flesh. Leave the flesh in a colander to drain for at least 30 minutes.

Meanwhile, heat the olive oil and sauté the garlic for a couple of minutes. Transfer to a food processor, add the vinegar, lemon juice, walnuts, some salt and the aubergine pulp and purée until smooth. (If not using a food processor, chop very finely.) Taste and season with extra salt and ground black pepper.

ASPARAGUS WITH DILL MAYONNAISE

For a really luxurious sandwich add some smoked salmon or cooked prawns and lots of lemon juice to this sandwich. This mayonnaise recipe makes more than you need but it keeps really well in the fridge in a screw-topped jar. It's delicious served with hot or cold fish.

SERVES 4, PREP 15 MINS, COOKING 5–10 MINS

FOR THE MAYONNAISE
1 whole egg
1 egg yolk
3 tbsp fresh lemon juice
3 tsp Dijon mustard
sea salt flakes and ground black pepper

350 ml / 12 fl oz sunflower oil
4 tbsp chopped fresh dill

350g/ 3/4 lb asparagus
4 pitta breads

Bring a large saucepan of water to the boil. Cook the asparagus until it is just done – overcooking will ruin it. Refresh with cold water immediately and leave to drain.

Make the mayonnaise, in a food processor, or in a bowl with a hand whisk, whisk together the egg and egg yolk. Add the lemon juice, mustard and a pinch of salt. Mix well. Very slowly, with the machine running or while whisking, add the oil drop by drop. When all the oil is incorporated, add the dill and season with salt and pepper. Slice open the pitta bread and spread some mayonnaise inside each one. Slide a quarter of the asparagus into each one. Serve.

BEETROOT WITH CREAM CHEESE AND HORSERADISH ON BAGELS

You should make sure the cooked beetroot you buy is not in vinegar – unless that's what you specifically want! Bagels are a sandwich staple. You can buy ones with different flavours such as onion or cinnamon (good toasted and spread generously with cream cheese). This sandwich also works very well, with cholla, a traditional Jewish bread available from some supermarkets.

SERVES 4, PREP 10 MINS

225 g / 8 oz cooked beetroot
175 g / 6 oz cream cheese
3–4 tsp horseradish

sea salt flakes and ground black pepper
4 bagels

Drain the beetroot and slice thinly. Blend the cream cheese with horseradish and season to taste. Halve the bagels horizontally, spread the cheese thickly on the bottom half and top with the beetroot. Cover with the bagel tops.

HERBY CHEESE WITH TOMATO

This may seem simple – but the best ideas always are! The tomatoes must be red, ripe and fragrant and this combination would work well with bagels or a nutty bread such as walnut bread. It takes no time at all to make and is very popular with kids – perfect for a packed lunch.

SERVES 4, PREP 10 MINS

125 g / 4 oz cream cheese with herbs
2 tbsp Greek yoghurt
sea salt and ground black pepper

4 rolls or bagels or 8 slices of bread
1 ripe beef tomato, thickly sliced

Mix together the cheese and yoghurt and season with salt and ground black pepper. Spread inside your bread and top with tomato slices. Put the lids on and wrap or serve!

BLT

My version, with a few twists! If you are not a huge fan of coriander, leave it out. If you're making this sandwich at home, try eating it while the bacon is still hot – it's delicious! Use the best quality bacon you can find – there are many specialist home-cured bacons available that make fantastic BLTs.

SERVES 4, PREP 10 MINS

1 ripe avocado
juice of 1/2 lime
a handful coriander leaves, roughly chopped
sea salt flakes and ground black pepper

8 slices granary bread
4 ripe tomatoes, thinly sliced
12 slices bacon, grilled until crispy
a handful fresh soft lettuce leaves
2 tbsp mayonnaise

Put the avocado, lime juice and coriander in a bowl, mash everything together and season well. Toast the bread under a preheated grill if you like, then spread four slices with the avocado mixture. Divide the tomato slices between the avocado mixture and top with the bacon and torn lettuce leaves. Spread the other four pieces of bread or toast with mayonnaise and use to cover the bacon to make sandwiches.

BRIE WITH LINGON

This is a really delicious combination. Lingon is a Swedish version of cranberry sauce – it is generally slightly tarter than most cranberry sauces but fruity nonetheless. A little watercress gives an added bite to the sandwich, whilst the oak leaf lettuce has a more delicate flavour. When choosing Brie make sure it is ripe: it should just give when pressed on the top and the edges should be glossy and creamy – if it looks at all hard and chalky it's not ripe.

SERVES 4, PREP 20 MINS

225 g / 8 oz ripe Brie
4 tbsp lingon relish
8 slices of multigrain bread

a handful of oak leaf lettuce leaves
a small bunch of watercress
sea salt flakes and ground black pepper

Thinly slice the Brie, cutting the vertical rind off. Spread the lingon between all the slices of bread. Arrange the Brie on four slices of the bread. Wash and dry the lettuce leaves. Divide between the sandwiches. Season and top with the remaining slices of bread.

BEEF WITH BEETROOT CHUTNEY

This is a perfect way to use up leftover roast beef. However, good sliced cooked beef is available from many specialist food shops and supermarket deli counters.

SERVES 4, PREP 15 MINS, COOKING 10 MINS

FOR THE BEETROOT CHUTNEY
5 tbsp redcurrant jelly
1 tbsp port
1 small raw beetroot, peeled

a pinch of freshly grated nutmeg
1 large baguette
8 thin slices of beef

To make the chutney, put the jelly, port and beetroot in a saucepan, cover and cook very gently until the jelly has dissolved. Simmer for 5 minutes until the mixture has thickened slightly. Allow to cool.

Cut the baguette into four, then slice each piece horizontally. Spread the chutney between the four bottom slices and sprinkle with a little nutmeg. Put two pieces of beef on top of each slice and top with the remaining bread. Serve.

BEEF WITH ROASTED AUBERGINE AND PEPPERS

Another recipe to use up cold roasted beef; perfect for Monday lunchtimes! Add a little mustard if you like. For a vegetarian option, leave out the beef and horseradish and spread the bread with tapenade. Use bought roasted peppers if you want to save time.

SERVES 4, PREP 10 MINS, COOKING 40 MINS

1 red pepper, seeded and roughly chopped
1 yellow pepper, seeded and roughly chopped
1 aubergine, sliced

2 tbsp olive oil
8 slices really fresh white bread
4 thickish slices cold roast beef
1 tbsp balsamic vinegar

Place the peppers and aubergine in a pan and sprinkle with oil. Roast in a preheated oven at 200 °C / 400 °F / gas mark 6, for 40 minutes. Allow to cool. Divide the peppers between four of the slices of bread and arrange a beef slice on top of each. Add the balsamic vinegar to the roasting pan, mix well, then drizzle the juices over the meat. Top each with another slice of bread. Store in the fridge but bring up to room temperature before serving.

ORIENTAL VEGETABLES WITH BLACK BEAN SAUCE

This is fab for veggies and for those watching their fat intake. It's best with a really fresh, soft, moist bread – especially one with onions in it – or in split pitta breads, which make it easier to eat.

SERVES 4, PREP 15 MINS

2 medium carrots, grated
50 g / 2 oz mangetout, blanched
75 g / 3 oz baby sweetcorn, blanched
and sliced diagonally into thirds
75 g / 3 oz beansprouts
8 slices of bread

FOR THE DRESSING
4 tbsp olive oil
1 tbsp dark soy sauce
2 tbsp black bean sauce
1 tbsp freshly squeezed lemon juice
2.5 cm / 1 in piece of root ginger,
peeled and crushed
sea salt flakes and ground black pepper

In a large bowl mix together the carrots, mangetout, sweetcorn, and beansprouts. To make the dressing thoroughly mix together all the ingredients. Pour the dressing over the vegetables and mix well. Divide between four slices of the bread and top with the remaining slices. Press down gently. Half and serve.

BANANA AND PEANUT BUTTER

This sandwich is very popular with kids. If you can't get chocolate bread, try spreading white bread with a thin layer of chocolate spread, with or without ground hazelnuts, to make a really naughty sandwich! Most people have a vehement preference for either smooth or crunchy peanut butter – it's up to you! Another good sweet sandwich idea is sliced bananas with butter on toasted raisin and cinnamon bread.

SERVES 4, PREP 5 MINS

4 tbsp peanut butter
8 slices chocolate bread
2 large bananas

Spread the peanut butter equally over all the slices of bread. Peel and diagonally slice the bananas and divide the slices between four slices of the bread. Top with the remaining slices of the bread. Press lightly together and cut in half.

BEEF WITH TARRAGON MAYONNAISE

Tarragon is one of my favourite herbs, I often put it with chicken, but it also works beautifully with beef.

SERVES 4, PREP 10 MINS, COOKING 10 MINS

knob of butter
1 dtsp oil
225 g / 8 oz fillet steak
4 tbsp hollandaise sauce from a jar
2 tbsp mayonnaise
1 dtsp fresh lemon juice

2 tbsp tarragon
sea salt flakes and ground black pepper
1 baguette
1 small cos lettuce

Melt the butter and the oil in heavy-based frying pan. Fry the steak about 4–5 minutes on each side. Leave to cool. Mix together the hollandaise sauce, mayonnaise, lemon juice and tarragon and season well. Cut the baguette into four and halve each piece horizontally. Spread the sauce between the baguette slices. Slice the steak thinly and divide between the sandwiches. Top with lettuce and serve.

BEEF WITH ROCKET AND BALSAMIC VINEGAR

This is yummy in a baguette. It's very simple but a great combination of ingredients. If you can get hold of wild rocket, use it. This filling would be good in a pain de campagne or a Parmesan cheese bread, if you can find them.

SERVES 4, PREP 5 MINS

4 ripe tomatoes, sliced
8 slices of crusty white bread
sea salt flakes and ground black pepper
8 slices of cooked beef

a large handful of baby rocket or wild rocket
balsamic vinegar to taste

Divide the tomatoe slices between four of the slices of bread. Season with salt and pepper and top with the beef slices, then the rocket. Sprinkle with balsamic vinegar to taste. Top each with a slice of bread, then press down lightly, cut in half and serve.

BUTTER-BEAN PÂTÉ WITH ROASTED PEPPERS AND CORIANDER

This butter-bean pâté will actually go with anything, not just peppers, juicy ripe tomatoes, grated carrot, roasted vegetables, beansprouts etc...

SERVES 4, PREP 15 MINS, COOKING 40 MINS

1 red pepper, seeded and thinly sliced
1 yellow pepper, seeded and thinly sliced
olive oil

FOR THE PÂTÉ
400 g / 14 oz tin butter-beans
3 tbsp extra virgin olive oil
2 cloves garlic, peeled and crushed

juice of one lemon
3 tbsp fresh coriander roughly chopped
pinch paprika
sea salt flakes and ground black pepper

8 slices of crusty white bread

Preheat the oven to 200 °C / 400 °F / gas mark 6. Put the peppers in a roasting pan, drizzle with oil and roast for 40 minutes.

Meanwhile, place all the pâté ingredients in a food processor and run the machine until smooth.

Remove the peppers from the oven, allow to cool slightly, then cut into strips. Spread pâté on the four of the slices of bread and top with the roasted peppers. Cover with the remaining slices of bread and serve. The pâté will keep in the fridge for 3–4 days.

AMERICAN CHICKEN WITH AVOCADO AND CHEDDAR

This is a classic American deli sandwich. It's very filling – a real meal in itself!

SERVES 4, PREP 15 MINS

2 cooked chicken breasts, skinned
4 tbsp mayonnaise
2 tbsp finely chopped flat leaf parsley
2 spring onions, finely sliced
sea salt and ground black pepper
pinch of paprika
8 slices granary bread

2 ripe tomatoes, sliced
1 ripe avocado, skinned, pitted and sliced
1 tbsp lemon juice
125 g / 4 oz sharp Cheddar cheese, grated

Thinly slice the chicken breasts and put into a bowl. Add the mayonnaise, parsley, spring onions and season with salt and pepper and paprika. Divide the mixture between four slices of the bread. Top with the tomato slices. Toss the avocado slices in the lemon juice and pile on top of the tomato. Divide the grated Cheddar between the sandwiches and put the remaining slices of bread on the top. Press down gently before cutting in half and packing into lunchboxes.

PLOUGHMAN'S SANDWICH

This is an updated version of a ploughman's lunch. By making use of all the fantastic quality ingredients that are available you can really elevate this simple combination to gourmet status. Use really fresh white bread – cut thickly, but not doorsteps. It's perfectly complemented by some good old-fashioned pickled onions! It's also nice using crisp apples, thinly sliced instead of or as well as, tomatoes.

SERVES 4, PREP 15 MINS

200 g / 7 oz mature Cheddar cheese, thinly sliced
4 slices bread
4 heaped tbsp good fruit chutney
4 vine ripened tomatoes

a handful of soft English lettuce leaves, washed and roughly torn
sea salt flakes and ground black pepper
6 radishes, thinly sliced (optional)

Arrange the cheese over four of the bread slices. Spread the chutney over the cheese. Top with the tomato, then lettuce, then radishes. Season to taste. Place the remaining bread slices on top of the sandwiches and press down gently before cutting in half.

CRAB WITH LEMON AND CHILLI

This is a really delicious crab recipe – it's also good served as a salad with hot toast. Pre-prepared crab is available from most fishmongers or supermarket fish counters. Try to use fresh rather than frozen.

SERVES 4, PREP 10 MINS (PLUS 30 MINS STANDING TIME)

juice of 2 lemons
2 tbsp white wine
4 tbsp extra virgin olive oil
3 fresh chillies, seeded and sliced
2 tbsp fresh dill, roughly chopped

sea salt flakes
225 g / 8 oz cooked crab meat
50 g / 2 oz bag of mixed leaves
8 slices of bread

Mix half of the lemon juice with the white wine, oil, chillies and dill, and season with sea salt. Pour over the crab meat and mix well. Leave it to marinate for at least half an hour. Arrange half the mixed leaves on four slices of bread, add the crab, top with the remaining leaves and bread slices.

SPANISH CHORIZO SANDWICH

In Spain bread served with a meal or with tapas is traditionally rubbed with garlic and fresh tomatoes. The addition of thinly sliced chorizo, a spicy Spanish sausage makes this into a wonderful sandwich. It keeps really well – the flavours just develop even more over time.

SERVES 4, PREP 10 MINS

4 garlic cloves, peeled
4 portions of crusty white bread;
something with a little rye would be
excellent

4 ripe tomatoes
olive oil for drizzling
12 thin slices chorizo sausage
sea salt and ground black pepper

Squash the garlic cloves with the blade of a knife and rub all over the cut sides of the bread. Slice each tomato in half and rub each half of tomato on a slice of bread. Really squash the flesh into the bread – you should be left with a piece of ragged tomato skin which you can throw away. Drizzle a little olive oil over each piece of bread. Arrange the chorizo over 4 slices and season with salt and pepper. Top with the remaining slices of bread and press firmly together before serving or wrapping for your lunchbox.

CRAB WITH TABASCO, TOMATO AND SOUR CREAM

This is quite a rich sandwich but fantastically good. It's best served in really fresh wholemeal bread. It's a good idea to pack a couple of extra wedges of lemon in your lunchbox.

SERVES 4, PREP 15 MINS

175 g / 6 oz crabmeat (either fresh, frozen and thawed or canned)
2 tbsp sour cream (plus extra for spreading)
juice of 1/2 lemon
1 spring onion
1 tsp Tabasco
sea salt flakes and ground black pepper
4 ripe beef tomatoes, thickly sliced
very finely chopped fresh flat leaf parsley, to garnish
8 slices of bread

Mix together the crabmeat, sour cream, lemon juice and spring onion. Season to taste with the Tabasco and salt and pepper. Spread a little extra sour cream on one side of each of the slices of bread, cover with the tomato slices, the crab mixture and parsley and top with another slice of bread.

CAMEMBERT WITH DATES AND APPLES

Fresh dates are readily available from supermarkets nowadays. If you can find the soft and sticky Medjool variety, they are simply delicious.

SERVES 4, PREP 10 MINS

225 g / 8 oz ripe Camembert
8 slices of bread
2 Cox's apples, cored and thinly sliced
1 tbsp lemon juice

8 fresh dates, chopped
1 head of soft English lettuce, washed and roughly torn
2 tbsp mayonnaise

Spread the cheese between four of the slices of bread. Toss the apple slices in the lemon juice and arrange over the Camembert. Sprinkle the dates over the cheese, then arrange the lettuce over the top. Spread the mayonnaise over the remaining slices of bread and use them to cover the sandwiches. Press down gently before cutting in half and wrapping for your lunchbox.

COTTAGE CHEESE WITH PINEAPPLE

This is really refreshing – a great light lunch especially for those watching their fat intake. It is particularly delicious made with a multigrain bread or good wholemeal. You could use drained canned pineapple but fresh really is so much nicer. For those of you short of time, fresh ready-prepared pineapple is available from most supermarkets.

SERVES 4, PREP 10 MINS

225 g / 8 oz cottage cheese
8 slices of bread
175 g / 6 oz fresh pineapple, sliced
50 g / 2 oz pine nuts, toasted

1 head of soft English lettuce, washed and roughly torn
sea salt flakes and ground black pepper

Spread the cottage cheese over four of the slices of bread and arrange the pineapple slices on top. Sprinkle with pine nuts, then arrange the lettuce over the top. Season lightly with salt and pepper and cover with the remaining slices of bread.

CHICKEN WITH SAFFRON MAYO AND RED PEPPERS

Saffron is my favourite spice. It is a good thing you only need a few strands to add flavour and colour to food as it is rather expensive.

SERVES 4, PREP 10 MINS

2 red peppers
1 tbsp boiling water
pinch saffron
4 tbsp mayonnaise
1 tbsp lemon juice
sea salt flakes and ground black pepper

8 slices bread
2 cooked chicken breasts, thinly sliced
a handful of crunchy lettuce leaves, such as cos or iceberg, washed and roughly torn

Halve and seed the peppers, remove the inner membranes, slice very thinly. Pour the boiling water over the saffron and leave for a couple of minutes. Mix the saffron and water with the mayonnaise, add the lemon juice and seasoning. Spread the mayonnaise over four of the slices of bread. Arrange the chicken slices, then the peppers over the top. Cover with the lettuce, then top with the remaining slices of bread. Press down gently before slicing in halves and wrapping or serving.

CORONATION CHICKEN SANDWICH

This is a really classic combination, always popular. It works well on white or granary bread, but something like raisin bread or naan could be fantastic. This is also a very easy way to make a curried mayonnaise.

SERVES 4, PREP 10 MINS

6 tbsp mayonnaise
2 tbsp mango chutney
sea salt flakes and ground black pepper
1 large banana
1 tbsp lemon juice
125 g / 4 oz black grapes

2 cooked chicken breasts, skinned and sliced
8 slices of bread
a small bunch of watercress, picked over and washed

Mix together the mayonnaise and chutney. Peel the banana and slice it diagonally, removing any brown bits or stringy pith, then douse the slices in lemon juice. Halve the grapes and remove the pips. Mix the chicken slices, banana and grapes into the mayonnaise mixture gently but thoroughly and season to taste. Divide this mixture between four of the slices of bread. Arrange the watercress over the top. Top with the remaining slices of bread. Press down gently before slicing in halves and packing into lunchboxes.

CHICKEN SATAY

Hot peanut sauce is really popular in Thai and Malaysian cuisine. This is a super-quick version and makes a really interestingly textured sandwich.

SERVES 4, PREP 20 MINS

FOR THE SATAY SAUCE
6 tbsp crunchy peanut butter
2 tsp Tabasco sauce
1/2 in piece of fresh ginger, peeled and crushed
2 tbsp lemon juice
1 tsp soy sauce

sea salt flakes and ground black pepper
8 slices of white bread or 4 pittas
2 cooked chicken breasts, skinned and thinly sliced
2 spring onions, finely chopped
1/2 cucumber, peeled and thinly sliced
175 g / 6 oz beansprouts

To make the satay sauce, mix together all the ingredients, seasoning to taste. Spread over all eight slices of the bread. Arrange the chicken over four slices of the bread and sprinkle over the spring onions. Top with the cucumber slices and beansprouts, then cover with the remaining slices of bread. Press down gently before cutting the sandwiches in half and packing into lunchboxes.

CHICKEN WITH TARRAGON, FRESH CHERRIES AND SOUR CREAM ON SOURDOUGH

This is a sandwich for the short cherry season. It's a lovely, fresh combination and works really well either on its own or with a big green salad and plenty of crusty sourdough bread for lunchtime entertaining. The cherries must be fresh not canned or glacé (that would be horrid!) Sourdough, a speciality of San Francisco, is readily available in most supermarkets and specialist bread shops. This kind of bread keeps well for three or four days as its flavour improves. Outside of the season, peeled and seeded cucumber can be substituted for the cherries.

SERVES 4, PREP 20 MINS

2 cooked chicken breasts, skinned, OR 275-350 g / 10–12 oz cooked chicken
6 tbsp sour cream
2 tbsp tarragon vinegar or lemon juice
2 tbsp mayonnaise
2 tbsp roughly chopped fresh tarragon

175 g / 6 oz fresh cherries, stoned and roughly chopped
sea salt flakes and ground black pepper
8 slices of sourdough bread
a handful of mild lettuce such as lambs' lettuce

Slice the chicken thinly and set aside. Mix together the sour cream, vinegar or lemon juice, mayonnaise and tarragon and season to taste. Mix in the cherries. Divide this mixture between four slices of the bread. Arrange the chicken over the cherries and top with the lettuce. Place the remaining slices of bread on top. Press down gently before cutting the sandwiches in half and wrapping for lunch-boxes or serving.

CAESAR SALAD SANDWICH

Caesar salad is a classic and it makes a delicious sandwich packed into a really fresh crusty baguette with shreds of chicken. Alternatively, if you want something more substantial, add a few slices of steak or fresh tuna. I feel like a bit of a cheat putting this recipe in the sandwich section as the salad is already written elsewhere, but I do not see the point in developing another Caesar salad recipe when this one is so scrumptious.

SERVES 4, PREP 15 MINS

FOR THE CAESAR SALAD
see recipe page 161
1 large fresh baguette, sliced
2 chicken breasts, cooked

Make the salad. Slice the baguette into four pieces and halve each piece horizontally. Pack the bottom of each with the salad. Shred the chicken and put on top of the salad. Cover with the top of the baguette and serve.

CHICKEN WITH PICKLED JALAPEÑO CHILLIES ON CORN BREAD

This has a distinct Mexican flavour to it.

SERVES 4, PREP 20 MINS, COOKING 10 MINS

2 chicken breasts, flattened with a rolling pin
2 tbsp olive oil
2 pickled jalapeño chillies, finely chopped
2 tbsp coriander leaves, roughly chopped

4 tbsp sour cream
sea salt flakes and ground black pepper
8 slices of corn bread, or a good granary
4 ripe tomatoes

Heat a griddle pan until really hot, brush the chicken breasts with the olive oil and cook for approximately 5 minutes on each side until done. Leave to cool, then slice thinly. Mix together the chillies, coriander and soured cream and season with salt and pepper. Spread the mixture over all eight slices of bread. Arrange the tomato slices over four of the slices of the bread. Top with the chicken slices and cover with the remaining slices of bread. Press down gently before cutting into halves and packing into lunchboxes.

DATES WITH CREAM CHEESE AND BANANA

The dates and bananas make this sandwich quite sweet. Choose medjool dates, they're definitely the best.

SERVES 4, PREP 5 MINS

4 bagels
125 g / 4 oz cream cheese
6 medjool dates, stoned and chopped

1 banana
ground cinnamon, to taste

Halve the bagels, spread each half with cream cheese and top with the dates. Peel and slice the banana and arrange on top of the dates. Sprinkle with a little cinnamon.

CLASSIC EGG MAYONNAISE WITH CRESS

Always use free-range eggs, you will notice a difference in taste. Keep the eggs at room temperature and bring the water to the boil before you add them to the pan. The eggs would continue to cook once they have been removed from the pan so make sure that you run them under cold water.

SERVES 4, PREP 15 MINS, COOKING 6 MINS

6 free-range eggs
sea salt flakes and ground black pepper
6 tbsp mayonnaise

8 slices of wholemeal or white bread
a handful of fresh cress
4 rashers bacon, grilled until crisp

Bring a pan of water to the boil, add the eggs and boil for 6 minutes. (This will give you soft-boiled eggs, that is the yolk will be slightly runny in the centre. If you prefer the yolk to be completely set, boil for 7 minutes.) Shell the eggs under a running cold tap. Place them in a clean, dry bowl, season and roughly mash with a fork, then leave the egg to cool. Add the mayonnaise and mix together. Spread the egg mayonnaise on four slices of bread and scatter over the fresh cress. Cut the bacon into little pieces and scatter over the cress. Top with another piece of bread, cut in half and serve.

EGG MAYONNAISE WITH SMOKED SALMON AND CHIVES

This is like an up-market scrambled egg. You may be familiar with the fabulous combination of scrambled egg and smoked salmon, but this is the version that goes inside a sandwich and travels.

SERVES 4, PREP 15 MINS, COOKING 6 MINS

5 eggs
sea salt flakes and ground black pepper
5 tbsp mayonnaise
a handful of fresh chives, roughly
chopped

125 g / 4 oz smoked salmon
4 or 8 slices of bread of your choice
juice of 1 lemon
lemon wedges, to serve

Bring a pan of water to the boil, add the eggs and boil for 6 minutes. Shell the eggs under cold running water and put them into a clean, dry bowl. Season and roughly mash with a fork, then leave the egg to cool. Add the mayonnaise and chives and mix together. Divide the salmon between the slices of bread, top with the egg mayonnaise and season well. Either cover with another piece of bread or leave open. Serve with wedges of lemon, for squeezing over the top.

FRENCH BEANS AND POACHED EGGS ON RYE BREAD

The combination of fresh beans, soft eggs and rye is too good to miss. It may not be very practical for a lunchbox, but it tastes delicious if you have time to pop home for lunch. Alternatively, eat this dish as a brunch, it's a cracker.

SERVES 4, PREP 10 MINS, COOKING 10 MINS

4 eggs
125 g / 4 oz fresh French beans
8 slices of rye bread

50 g / 2 oz butter
sea salt flakes and ground black pepper

Bring a large frying pan of water just to the boil. Break the eggs one at a time into a cup and slide into the water. Cook for one minute (use a timer for accuracy). Turn off the heat, cover and leave the eggs for 10 minutes, basting them with the water occasionally to make sure that they are covered at all times. Meanwhile, bring a pan of water to the boil, add the beans and blanch for a few minutes. Put the bread on four plates, spread with the butter, top with a few crisp beans and rest a poached egg on top. Season well.

MEDITERRANEAN FENNEL AND PEPPER

I have been served fennel in Italy at the end of a meal. I didn't like to say anything at the time, but I prefer little sticks of fennel at the beginning of a meal with lots of yummy dips or as part of the main course. Raw and cooked fennel have quite different flavours. Raw fennel is crisp and juicy with a liquorice flavour while roasted fennel is sweet and creamy in comparison.

SERVES 4, PREP 15 MINS

1 fennel bulb
1 small sun-dried tomato loaf
4 tbsp black olive paste or sun-dried tomato paste

3 red peppers, seeded, roasted and thinly sliced
4 tbsp mayonnaise
sea salt flakes and ground black pepper

Halve the fennel lengthways, then slice thinly into little strips. Cut the bread into eight thin slices. Spread four of the slices with the olive or sun-dried tomato paste, top with the sliced peppers, fennel slices and mayonnaise. Season to taste. Put the remaining slices of bread on top and wrap in greaseproof paper or place in bags.

FIGS WITH KELSTON PARK CHEESE

Kelston Park cheese is gooey and soft. It's made from double cream and has all the indulgent qualities associated with this ingredient. It really doesn't need much else served with it, but it is rather good with fresh figs. If you have trouble finding Kelston Park cheese use another soft cheese of your choice.

SERVES 4, PREP 5 MINS

4 fresh figs
125 g / 4 oz Kelston Park cheese
4 soft bread rolls

Cut the figs in half, top each with a thick slice of Kelston Park cheese and put into the middle of a soft bread roll. Enjoy.

FETA WITH TAPENADE, RED AND YELLOW TOMATOES

A sandwich with a Greek influence, from our friend Feta cheese. Feta is quite salty, so go carefully on seasoning. I love using red and yellow tomatoes together; apart from the obvious colour difference, their different flavours really complement one another. If you don't like tapenade use sundried tomato paste, instead.

SERVES 4, PREP 15 MINS

8 slices crusty bread
4 tbsp black olive tapenade
4 ripe red tomatoes, thinly sliced
4 ripe yellow tomatoes, thinly sliced

150 g / 5 oz Feta cheese
a handful of fresh flat leaf parsley, roughly chopped
a little garlic mayonnaise (optional)

Spread all of the slices of bread with the tapenade. Lay the tomatoes over four of the bread slices. Crumble the Feta on top, scatter over fresh parsley and cover with the other slices of bread. Serve with garlic mayonnaise if you like.

GOAT'S CHEESE WITH MUSHROOMS ON FOCCACIA

I have learnt that, as a general rule, people either love or hate goat's cheese. There is no in between. If you fall into the latter category, use a different cheese. It works really well with a blue cheese.

SERVES 4, PREP 15 MINS, COOKING 5 MINS

150 g / 5 oz goat's cheese
4 foccacia slices or walnut bread
a handful of fresh chives
1 tbsp olive oil
2 garlic cloves, peeled and sliced

150 g / 5 oz field mushrooms, thinly sliced
2 tbsp French dressing
a handful of walnuts, toasted and roughly chopped (optional)

Spread the cheese on four of the slices of bread and sprinkle the chives over. Heat the oil in a frying pan and sauté the garlic for a few minutes. Add the mushrooms and cook for a couple of minutes. If you are eating this sandwich straight away, top the cheese with the warm mushrooms immediately: otherwise, leave them to cool before dividing between the bread and cheese. Drizzle the dressing over the top and scatter with the walnuts if using. Cover with the other slices of bread, and wrap up or serve.

Humus with Roasted Aubergine, Lemon Juice and Roasted Red Peppers in Pitta

If you need to be really quick, use bought humus and roasted peppers and aubergines from your supermarket deli.

Serves 4, Prep 15 mins

8 tbsp humus (see page 140)
8 slices bread of your choice
8 slices roasted aubergine
(see page 131)
8 slices roasted red peppers
(see page 141)

juice of 1 lemon
1 tbsp extra virgin olive oil
sea salt flakes and ground black pepper
a handful of fresh flat leaf parsley,
roughly chopped

Spread the humus on four slices of the bread. Top with slices of roasted aubergine and pepper. Mix together the lemon juice, olive oil and seasoning. Drizzle the dressing over the peppers and scatter over the parsley. Top each with another slice of bread, wrap up and go.

HERRINGS ON RYE BREAD WITH SOUR CREAM AND DILL

Herrings with soured cream and apples is a Scandinavian combination. It is best to chill this sandwich before eating to make it perfect for the lunchbox. There are so many different pickled or marinated herrings to choose from nowadays, make sure that for something like this you choose the plain pickled herrings or herrings in sour cream rather than those that come in thick and rich sauces. If you use herrings already in sour cream, you may like to add slightly less than the measure suggested here. See how you feel.

SERVES 4, PREP 10 MINS

1/2 cucumber
400 g / 14 oz pickled herrings
50 ml / 2 fl oz sour cream
2 tart apples, peeled, cored and thinly sliced

sea salt flakes and ground black pepper
a handful of fresh dill, roughly chopped
8 slices of rye bread

Halve the cucumber lengthways, scoop out the seeds and cut the flesh into bite-sized pieces. Chop the herrings into small pieces and place in a bowl. Add the sour cream, apple slices and cucumber and mix everything together. Season well, add the dill and spoon on to four pieces of the rye bread. Top with the other four.

HAM, GORGEOUS RIPE BRIE AND BABY SPINACH

In Italy, coffee bars are similar to mini delis and they often serve panini – sandwiches containing ingredients like cheese and ham that are made in advance and then grilled to order. This recipe was inspired by panini. The combination of cheese and ham is so delicious. If you are able to grill the sandwich before serving, great, if not: it will still taste good.

SERVES 4, PREP 10 MINS, COOKING 10 MINS

8 slices of white bread
25 g / 1 oz butter
4 slices of ham
1 ripe brie

a little mayonnaise
50 g / 2 oz baby spinach leaves,
roughly chopped
sea salt flakes and ground black pepper

Spread the bread with the butter and arrange the ham on four of the slices. Top with slices of Brie. Dot each with a little mayonnaise and scatter over the spinach leaves. Season to taste. Cover with the other slices of buttered bread. Serve as they are or heat a griddle pan until really hot, place a sandwich on and weigh it down with a heavy frying pan. Brown the sandwich, turn over and repeat on the other side. Cut in half and serve hot.

HAM AND GRUYÈRE WITH DIJON MUSTARD

This is similar to the previous recipe in the sense that it is also delicious served cold or grilled and served hot. Avoid pre-packed slices of ham, they often contain added water and preservatives. Most supermarkets now sell a good selection of ham off the bone that can be sliced to your required thickness. Otherwise, pop into your local deli. Mustard is always a good addition when you are making ham sandwiches – the heat of the mustard just sets off the ham perfectly.

SERVES 4, PREP 10 MINS

8 slices of bread
25 g / 1oz butter
8 slices good quality ham
8 thin slices Gruyère cheese

2 dtsp Dijon mustard
2 large beef tomatoes, thinly sliced
sea salt flakes and ground black pepper

Spread the bread with the butter and top four of the slices with two slices of ham, then two slices of cheese. Spread a little mustard over each, then arrange the tomato slices over the top and season. Cover with the other slices of buttered bread and serve as they are or heat a griddle pan until really hot, place a sandwich on and weigh it down with a heavy frying pan. Brown the sandwich, turn over and repeat on the other side. Cut in half and serve hot.

HONEY-ROAST HAM WITH MANGO MUSTARD

This is a little more unusual than a normal mayonnaise, I have used fresh mango to give the mayonnaise its thick texture and the oil creates its creaminess. The curry powder and cayenne pepper in the mayonnaise are brilliant with ham, however it also works well with cooked chicken breast.

SERVES 4, PREP 15 MINS

FOR THE MANGO MUSTARD
1 mango, peeled and stoned
4 tsp Dijon mustard
2 tsp white wine vinegar
juice of 1/2 lime
1 garlic clove, peeled and roughly chopped
50 ml / 2 fl oz olive oil

1/4 tsp cayenne pepper
1/4 tsp curry powder
sea salt flakes, to taste

8 slices granary bread
8 slices honey-roast ham
50 g / 2 oz mixed lettuce leaves, roughly torn

To make the mango and mustard mayonnaise, put the mango in a food processor and run the machine until soft, or mash with a fork. Add the mustard, vinegar, lime juice and garlic and mix together. Slowly whisk in the oil until emulsified. Add the cayenne and curry powder and season to taste with salt. Spread a little of the mayonnaise on each slice of bread, top four of the slices with the ham, then some of the crispy lettuce leaves and season well.

HOT DOGS WITH YELLOW MUSTARD, SAUTÉED ONIONS AND TOMATOES

This may seem rather odd for a lunchbox, but I had many requests from friends for sandwiches with sausages inside them. And what better way to eat sausages than with fried onions and mustard?

SERVES 4, PREP 10 MINS, COOKING 15 MINS

4 large juicy sausages
15 ml / 1 tbsp oil
2 Spanish onions, peeled and sliced

4 bread rolls of your choice
2 dtsp English mustard
2 ripe tomatoes, thinly sliced

Preheat the grill to high and cook the sausages until golden on the outside and cooked in the middle. Meanwhile, heat oil in a frying pan and fry the onions until golden and sticky (they need to cook for at least 15 minutes to give their sugar time to caramelise). Cut a slit in the middle of each of the rolls and spread with the mustard. Put a couple of tomato slices into the rolls, followed by the sausages and onions. Eat or leave to go cold and eat later.

LAMB WITH ONIONS, SPICES AND PISTACHIO MAYONNAISE IN PITTA

If you have had roast lamb at the weekend, this one is for you. If you haven't, remember this idea for next time and make sure you keep some cooked lamb for this sandwich. Alternatively, if you like the idea of this combination so much, cook a piece of lamb for the recipe. It is well worth the effort, especially if you are making it for a few people. As with all of the sandwiches in this book, you can very easily double or halve the quantity of the ingredients as necessary.

SERVES 4, PREP 15 MINS, COOKING 15 MINS

1 tsp cumin seeds
15 ml / 1 tbsp oil
2 Spanish onions, peeled and sliced
4 pitta breads

350 g / 12 oz sliced roasted lamb
a large handful of pistachios, roughly chopped
3 tbsp mayonnaise

Heat a frying pan, add the cumin seeds and dry-fry for a few minutes. Crush the seeds with a pestle and mortar. Heat the oil in the same pan, add the crushed seeds and the onions and fry for 15 minutes. Slice each pitta lengthways and fill with the lamb and the hot, spicy onions. Mix together the pistachios and mayonnaise and spoon into the breads. Serve warm or leave to cool and keep in the fridge until later.

MUSHROOMS FRIED IN GARLIC WITH ROQUEFORT IN A BAGUETTE

Unlike most blue cheeses, Roquefort is made from sheep's milk rather than cow's. It has a wonderful flavour and the characteristic blue veins associated with the other blue cheeses. Roquefort is aged for at least two months in the limestone caves of Cambalou in the South of France. When the cheese is first cut it looks white on the inside but after it is exposed to air, the characteristic blue veins appear. My husband and I have spent many evenings eating Roquefort, walnuts and walnut bread. When we have a little more time, we have also eaten the combination as given here. The filled baguettes can also be eaten cold, but must say that I prefer them warm.

SERVES 4, PREP 10 MINS, COOKING 10 MINS

25 g / 1 oz butter
5 large field mushrooms, thickly sliced
125 g / 4 oz Roquefort cheese

4 small baguettes
a handful of walnuts, lightly toasted

Heat the butter in a heavy-based frying pan, add the mushrooms and sauté for a few minutes. Crumble the Roquefort into the pan and toss everything together until the cheese is just melted. Slice the baguettes horizontally and spoon in the cheese and mushrooms. Serve immediately either with the walnuts handed separately to munch on at the same time or with them pushed into the sandwiches.

MOZZARELLA ON CIABATTA WITH RIPE TOMATOES, TORN BASIL AND OLIVE OIL

If you cannot get hold of ciabatta, use a fresh French stick. It is always the simplest things in life that are the best.

SERVES 4, PREP 15 MINS

1 large fresh ciabatta bread stick
2 tbsp extra virgin olive oil
1 Mozzarella ball, sliced
6 ripe tomatoes, vine ripened

2 tbsp balsamic vinegar
a handful of fresh basil leaves, roughly torn

Halve the ciabatta horizontally and drizzle each half with the extra virgin olive oil. Arrange the Mozzarella and tomato slices on the bottom half of the ciabatta. Drizzle over the balsamic vinegar and scatter the basil leaves over the top. Season to taste, cut into slices and serve immediately or wrap in greaseproof paper and take with you, wherever you may be going.

CREAMY SMOKED MACKEREL AND CUCUMBER ON A HERB FOCACCIA

A creamy, tasty sandwich – with hardly an ounce of fat in sight! This mackerel pâté is a favourite every time I serve it. It is so easy to make. If you ever find yourself without lunch or supper, make some of this satisfying and nutritious pâté and eat it with lots of fresh toast and salad.

SERVES 4, PREP 15 MINS

2 smoked mackerel fillets, skinned
1 tbsp creamed horseradish
125 ml / 4 fl oz natural yoghurt
2 cloves garlic, peeled

juice of 1/2 lemon
ground black pepper
1 herb focaccia loaf
1/2 cucumber, sliced

Put the mackerel, horseradish, yoghurt, garlic and the juice of 1/2 lemon into a food processor, purée until smooth. Season with pepper. Halve the focaccia horizontally and spread one half thickly with the pâté. Arrange the cucumber slices on top, and cover with the remaining foccacia. Cut into slices, wrap in greaseproof paper and away you go!

SMOKED MACKEREL ON RYE BREAD WITH HORSERADISH AND APPLE

Smoked fish is quite salty, so I season these sandwiches with ground black pepper only, not sea salt. There is something about creamed horseradish and smoked mackerel – the flavour combination is perfect. Choose little Cox's apples if they are in season, otherwise go for a sweet and crunchy apple, preferably with a good skin so that it can be left on.

SERVES 4, PREP 10 MINS

4 smoked mackerel fillets, skinned
2–3 tbsp creamed horseradish
8 slices rye bread

3 apples, cored and sliced
juice of 1 lime
ground black pepper

Flake the fish into large pieces. Spread the horseradish on to four pieces of the rye bread. Top with the flaked mackerel. Toss the apple slices in a bowl with the lime juice, then arrange on top of the fish and season with pepper. Top with the other slices of rye bread and wrap in paper.

PEAR, STILTON AND BACON ON WALNUT BREAD

The sweet and crunchy pears are perfect with the salty, crumbly Stilton and crisp bacon. Use walnut bread if you can get it, otherwise use granary bread and throw in a handful of chopped walnuts. Incidentally, streaky bacon crisps better than other cuts and tends to be more successful as a sandwich filling ingredient. But if you are vegetarian, omit the bacon altogether. This combination also makes a delicious salad if you substitute potatoes for the bread. All you need to do is boil 225 g / 8 oz new potatoes and roughly chop. Add the potatoes to a bowl with the other ingredients, mix well and serve.

SERVES 4, PREP 10 MINS, COOKING 10 MINS

5 rashers bacon
225 g / 8 oz Stilton, crumbled
2 pears, deseeded and sliced

a handful of walnuts, roughly chopped
4 tbsp Greek yoghurt
8 slices of walnut bread

Dry-fry the bacon until crispy. Drain on kitchen paper and cut into bite-sized pieces. Spread the Stilton over four slices of the bread, scatter over the pear slices and walnuts, if using, and the bacon pieces. Top with a spoonful of Greek yoghurt and cover with the remaining bread slices. Squeeze the sandwich together and wrap in greaseproof paper.

PRAWN COCKTAIL ON WHITE BREAD

Freshly boiled prawns from the seaside are rare today, which is a shame, but whole cooked prawns are the next best thing. Despite the fact that they will have been frozen, when you have removed the shells from the prawns they are more than acceptable.

Remember to keep the sandwich refrigerated until you are ready to eat. If you are concerned about the bread going soft, take the prawn cocktail in a separate container and assemble the sandwich with the bread and lettuce just before you are ready to eat.

SERVES 4, PREP 15 MINS

2 little gem lettuces, washed and torn into bite-size pieces
8 slices of white bread
2 spring onions, trimmed and thinly sliced
1/2 cucumber, seeded and thinly sliced
450 g / 1 lb cooked whole prawns, shelled

125 ml / 4 fl oz mayonnaise
2 tbsp tomato ketchup
4-5 drops Tabasco
1 tbsp Cognac (optional)
1 tbsp lemon juice
a pinch of paprika
2 lemons, cut into chunks

Divide the lettuce between four of the pieces of bread. Scatter over the spring onions and cucumber slices. Pile the prawns on top. Mix together the mayonnaise, tomato sauce, Tabasco, Cognac if using and lemon juice until the mixture is pink. Spoon on top of the prawns. Season to taste. Dust each with paprika and squeeze a little lemon juice over the top. Cover with the remaining slices of bread and wrap in greaseproof paper. Serve with the lemon to squeeze over.

PRAWNS WITH ORANGE SEGMENTS AND CRUNCHY LETTUCE

It may seem slightly extravagant, but I feel that 450 g / I lb of fresh cooked prawns to feed four people at lunchtime is perfectly justifiable, as long as it is not every day. The fresh orange cuts through the prawns and is a welcome change to lemon. The combination of yoghurt and mayonnaise acts as a barrier to the wet orange and prawns, stopping the bread from going soft.

SERVES 4, PREP 15 MINS

4 tbsp yoghurt
4 tbsp thick and creamy mayonnaise
8 slices of bread (your choice)
1/2 crunchy lettuce, finely shredded
450 g / I lb cooked whole prawns,
shells removed

I large juicy orange
a handful of fresh parsley, roughly
chopped

Mix together the yoghurt and mayonnaise and spread on the slices of bread. Arrange the lettuce and prawns over the top. Use a sharp knife to cut the top and bottom off the orange and then work your way around the fruit, slicing away the skin and white pith. Slice the orange flesh thinly into rounds and arrange on the prawns. Scatter the fresh parsley over, top with the other slice of bread and serve or wrap up and keep until lunchtime.

PRAWNS WITH CRISPY BACON AND PARSLEY

This combination of prawns and crispy bacon is just delicious. It is quite indulgent to have mayonnaise as well, but it is definitely needed. The crushed pink peppercorns are a visual change to black, however they should be used sparingly as they have a strong flavour.

SERVES 4, PREP 10 MINS, COOKING 15 MINS

4 rashers streaky bacon
4 tbsp mayonnaise
4 bread rolls of your choice
225 g / 8 oz cooked whole prawns, shelled

a few pink peppercorns, crushed
a handful of flat leaf parsley, roughly chopped

Dry-fry the bacon until crispy, then drain on kitchen paper and cut into little pieces. Spread the mayonnaise into the rolls and fill with the prawns and bacon. Scatter over a little crushed pink peppercorns and flat leaf parsley. Wrap up and keep or serve.

PROSCIUTTO WITH BROAD BEAN PURÉE

Only hams that carry the stamp of Ducal Crown are genuine *Prosciutto di Parma*, these have a really unique and subtle taste. The very best pork is used and it is bred in clearly defined areas to particular standards and then cured and assessed according to a recipe that has stood the test of time. So look for the stamp when you chose your slices of Prosciutto for this sandwich. If broad beans are not in season use frozen, they are normally quite young and sweet when frozen.

SERVES 4, PREP 10 MINS, COOKING 10 MINS

125 g / 4 oz broad beans
1 tbsp olive oil
1 1/2 tbsp Dijon mustard

sea salt flakes and ground black pepper
8 slices of bread
8 slices wafer thin Prosciutto di Parma

Cook the beans in boiling water until tender. Leave to cool then peel. Put the beans in a bowl, add the oil and mustard and mash to a purée. Season to taste and spread on to four of the slices of bread. Top the purée with a couple of pieces of ham. Cover with the remaining slices of bread, cut in half and serve or wrap up and keep until later.

PORK WITH CARAMELISED APPLES

This apple sauce tastes delicious and is incredibly easy and if you keep it covered it will last for several days in the fridge. All you need to do is cook pork for Sunday lunch or supper and keep some for these sandwiches. Cooked chicken can also be used.

If you want this to be even easier, buy a jar of caramelised apple compote from the Bay Tree Food Company.

SERVES 4, PREP 15 MINS, COOKING 10 MINS

FOR THE APPLE SAUCE
6 large apples, peeled and cored
juice of 2 lemons
125 ml / 4 fl oz apple juice
75 g / 3 oz golden caster sugar
3 tbsp marmalade

8 slices of crusty white bread
4 slices of cooked pork plus some crackling
sea salt flakes and ground black pepper

To make the apple sauce, put the apples into a bowl with the lemon juice and toss together. Put the apple juice, sugar and marmalade into a saucepan and bring to the boil, stirring constantly, until the sugar dissolves. Reduce the heat and simmer gently for about 5 minutes until syrupy. Add the apples and cook until soft. Transfer the apples to a bowl with a slotted spoon and mash until smooth. Reduce the syrup until thick, and blend into the apples. Leave the sauce to cool unless you are eating the sandwiches straight away. Spread the sauce thickly on to eight slices of the bread, top four of the slices with the pork and crackling. Season to taste, cover with the remaining slices of bread and serve.

BARBECUE GRIDDLED PORK WITH RED CABBAGE SLAW

This is delicious served hot or cold. This variation on coleslaw is crispy with a sweet barbecue flavour.

SERVES 4, PREP 20 MINS, COOKING 20 MINS

75 ml / 3 fl oz barbecue sauce
5 tbsp orange marmalade
50 ml / 2 fl oz hot pepper sauce
75 ml / 3 fl oz mayonnaise
2 tbsp mustard

1 tsp sugar
250 g / 9 oz red cabbage, shredded
sea salt flakes and ground black pepper
2 pork tenderloins, trimmed of any fat
4 bread rolls, cut in half

In a small bowl, mix together the barbecue sauce, marmalade and hot pepper sauce. In a separate bowl, whisk together the mayonnaise, half of the barbecue mixture, the mustard and sugar. Add the cabbage and stir to combine. Season to taste, cover and refrigerate for 1 hour. Brush the pork with the remaining barbecue sauce. Heat a griddle pan until hot and grill the meat for 5 minutes on each side. Continue to cook, turning occasionally, for about 20 minutes until the meat is cooked all the way through. Transfer the pork to a cutting board and slice thinly, cutting across the grain at a slight angle. Pile the warm sliced pork on the bottom of the bread rolls and top with the chilled slaw. Cover with the top halves of the rolls and serve. If you are not eating these immediately, leave the pork to cool slightly before covering with the top half of the rolls.

PRAWNS WITH LIME AND COCONUT DRESSING

This is a really zingy, fresh dressing which works really well with prawns, although it would also be good with cooked chicken, fresh tuna or fresh crab. You can use any left over coconut milk to make a smoothie (see page 264)

SERVES 4, PREP 10 MINS

FOR THE DRESSING
zest and juice of one lime
4 tbsp coconut milk
1 tbsp coriander leaves, roughly chopped
1 red chilli, seeded and finely chopped
2 tbsp mayonnaise

275 g / 10 oz fresh or frozen prawns
sea salt flakes and ground black pepper
8 slices of bread
1/2 cucumber, peeled and thinly sliced diagonally
2 baby gem lettuces

To make the dressing, mix together the lime zest and juice, coconut milk, coriander, chilli and mayonnaise. Put the prawns in a bowl and mix through the dressing. Season to taste. Pile the prawn mixture on to four of the slices of bread and top with the cucumber slices, then the lettuce leaves. Gently press the remaining slices of the bread on the top and then cut into two, wrap in greaseproof paper and pack into lunchboxes.

HERBY RICOTTA WITH ROASTED VEGETABLES

This is a simple but delicious sandwich. If you want a bit more punch try adding some freshly grated Parmesan or Pecorino cheese to the herbed ricotta before spreading it on to the bread.

SERVES 4, PREP 15 MINS

4 tbsp roughly chopped fresh herbs, such as basil, flat leaf parsley, rosemary
225 g / 8 oz Ricotta cheese
sea salt flakes and ground black pepper

a selection of roasted vegetables (see page 139)
4 ciabatta rolls

Mix the herbs with the ricotta and season well. Spread over the rolls and top with the vegetables. This is best wrapped and chilled in the refrigerator for a couple of hours to allow the flavours to develop.

SPINACH, CREAM CHEESE AND FRESH NUTMEG IN FLOUR TORTILLAS

Fresh spinach, cream cheese and nutmeg may be a classic combo but wrapped up in flour tortillas and warmed through, it takes on a whole new identity.

SERVES 4, PREP 15 MINS, COOKING 10 MINS

4 flour tortillas
125 g / 4 oz cream cheese
100 g / 3 oz fresh baby spinach leaves, roughly torn

1 whole nutmeg
sea salt flakes and ground black pepper

Preheat the oven to 180 °C / 350 °F / gas mark 4. Spread the tortillas with the cream cheese, scatter the fresh spinach leaves over the top of each and grate fresh nutmeg over. Season to taste and roll up each tortilla. Wrap in foil. Throw in the oven for 10 minutes to warm through before you eat.

SALMON WITH GREEN CHILLI MAYONNAISE ON BAGEL

You could use other fish, but salmon is a favourite of mine and it is so easy to get hold of. This recipe was inspired by a roll I ate in a restaurant in America. The crunchy salmon and cool chilli mayonnaise inside a soft roll tasted so good that I just had to include something similar here. I must confess, I have only ever eaten it still warm, as I have never managed to keep one long enough to see what it is like cold. You will need to try that yourselves if you wish to take this one away with you.

SERVES 4, PREP 10 MINS, COOKING 8 MINS

2 eggs
2 tbsp milk
4 tbsp plain flour
sunflower oil, for shallow-frying
4 salmon fillets, skinned
1 bag corn chips, crushed
(approx. 150 g / 5 oz)

4 soft bread rolls or bagels
1 green chilli, seeded and finely sliced
4 tbsp mayonnaise
2 tbsp yoghurt
juice of $1/2$ lime
sea salt flakes and ground black pepper

Mix together the eggs and milk. Put the flour in a separate bowl. Heat the oil in a large frying pan. Dip the salmon fillets into the flour, then the egg, then the crushed corn chips, coating them thickly. Add the fillets to the pan of oil and cook for about 4 minutes on each side until golden on the outside and cooked in the middle. Remove the fish from the pan with a slotted spoon and drain on kitchen paper. Transfer to the bottom halves of the rolls or bagels. Mix the chilli into the mayonnaise with the yoghurt and lime juice, stir really well and season. Top the salmon with the mayonnaise, then cover with the tops of the rolls.

SUBMARINE SANDWICHES

Delis all over the world are known for their submarine sandwiches. Pile it high with everything except the kitchen sink. Well, maybe not that much! This is perfect if you have hungry men to feed. That may seem like a sexist comment, but none of my girlfriends have ever eaten a whole one, they always share.

SERVES 4, PREP 10 MINS

FOR THE VINAIGRETTE
juice of 1 lemon
4 tbsp extra virgin olive oil
sea salt flakes and ground black pepper

1 French stick
3 tbsp mayonnaise
3 ripe tomatoes, thinly sliced
125 g / 4 oz prosciutto

175 g / 6 oz salami
100 g / 3¹/₂ oz Cheddar cheese, grated
175 g / 6 oz honey-roast ham, thinly sliced
125 g / 4 oz Provolone
12 pickled peppers
a handful of lettuce leaves

To make the vinaigrette dressing; put the ingredients into a screw-top jar and shake well.

Halve the loaf lengthways. Spread each half with mayonnaise, lay the tomato slices on the bottom half, then cover with the prosciutto, salami, Cheddar, ham, provolone and pickled peppers. Shred the lettuce and arrange on top. Drizzle with the vinaigrette and put the top on.

STEAK SANDWICH WITH WORCESTERSHIRE SAUCE

Delicious hot or cold. Add mustard and mayonnaise if you want, but just tender steak and fresh crisp watercress is fine by me.

SERVES 4, PREP 10 MINS, COOKING 5–10 MINS

25 g / 1 oz butter
2 tbsp olive oil
4 fillet steaks
4 mini white baguettes

50 g / 2 oz fresh watercress, roughly torn
sea salt flakes and ground black pepper
Worcestershire sauce, to serve

Melt the butter with the oil in a frying pan, add the steak and cook for a few minutes until golden brown. Turn the steak over and cook for another few minutes, to your taste. Leave to rest for a couple of minutes, then slice into strips. Slit the baguettes down the middle without cutting all the way through. Fill with the fresh watercress, followed by the steak slices. Drizzle over the juices from the pan. Season to taste and serve with Worcestershire sauce.

SMOKED SALMON MASHED WITH CREAM CHEESE AND SERVED WITH LEMON

This is just easy, quick and, above all, delicious.

SERVES 4, PREP 10 MINS

175 g / 6 oz smoked salmon trimmings
200 g / 7 oz cream cheese
1 tbsp lemon juice

sea salt flakes and ground black pepper
4 bread rolls
1 cucumber
1 lemon, cut into wedges

Shred the salmon into little pieces. Mix together the cream cheese, lemon juice and seasoning. Refrigerate until needed. Halve the cucumber lengthways and scoop out the seeds with a spoon. Finely dice the flesh. Spoon the cheese mixture into the rolls, add the cucumber and salmon. Season well and serve with the lemon wedges.

SARDINES, FENNEL, PARSLEY AND LEMON

Every time I have had a sardine sandwich it has been accompanied by a glass of cold beer. The two do seem to go well together.

SERVES 4, PREP 10 MINS

8 slices of bread
2 tbsp butter, softened
100 g / 3¹/₂ oz can sardines in oil,
drained
¹/₂ red onion, peeled and sliced

1 ripe tomato, thinly sliced
sea salt flakes and ground black pepper
1 lettuce, roughly torn
1 lemon, cut into wedges

Spread the bread with the butter. Mash the sardines in a bowl with lots of seasoning and spread on four of the slices of bread. Top the sardines with the onion and tomato slices. Scatter the lettuce over the top and season. Squeeze lemon juice over. Cover with the remaining slices of bread and serve with the lemon wedges.

GOAT'S CHEESE WITH ROSEMARY, ORANGE AND LEMON

This is perfect for taking to work or on a picnic and spreading straight on crisp French bread just before you are ready to eat. Serve with or without the turkey, as you wish.

SERVES 4, PREP 10 MINS (PLUS AT LEAST 1 HOUR MARINATING TIME)

200 g / 7 oz goat's cheese
zest of 1 lemon
zest of 1 orange

4 tbsp extra virgin olive oil
a sprig of rosemary
1 cooked turkey breast, shredded

Put the cheese in a dish, cover with the lemon and orange zest, oil and rosemary. Leave to marinate for at least 1 hour. Spread the cheese thickly on crusty French bread, top with the thin strips of turkey if using. Eat.

TURKEY WITH LINGONBERRY RELISH AND WATERCRESS

Substitute cranberry sauce if you cannot find lingonberry relish. These sandwiches look very attractive with the cream-coloured turkey next to the red sauce and bright green watercress.

SERVES 4, PREP 20 MINS

2 cooked turkey breasts, finely diced
4 tbsp mayonnise
6 tbsp Greek yoghurt
a pinch of paprika
sea salt flakes and ground black pepper

2 tbsp lingonberry relish
8 thin slices of bread
50 g / 2 oz fresh watercress, roughly chopped

Mix together the turkey, add the mayonnaise and yoghurt. Season with the paprika, salt and pepper. Spread the lingonberry relish on four slices of the bread, top with the turkey mixture, then the watercress. Put the remaining slices of bread on top, cut and serve or wrap in greaseproof paper.

TUNA MAYONNAISE WITH TOMATO

Everyone loves this combination so much that I felt obliged to include it in this book. If you want to make any changes, I do recommend thinly sliced strips of cucumber or spring onions as an alternative to tomato and lettuce.

SERVES 4, PREP 15 MINS

2 x 200g / 7 oz cans tuna in sunflower oil, drained
5–6 tbsp mayonnaise
1 red onion, peeled and finely diced
juice of $1/2$ lemon

sea salt flakes and ground black pepper
4 bread rolls
butter, for spreading
3 large ripe beef tomatoes, thinly sliced
a handful of shredded lettuce

Mix together the tuna, mayonnaise, onion, lemon juice and seasoning in a bowl. Slice the rolls in half and butter. Fill with the tuna mixture, top with a few slices of tomato and a little of the shredded lettuce.

TUNA MAYONNAISE, CHILLI AND CHEESE

A twist on the previous recipe. Seeing as tuna mayonnaise is always such a big hit I thought it deserved at least one variation.

SERVES 4, PREP 15 MINS

200 g / 7 oz can tuna in sunflower oil, drained
75 g / 3 oz Cheddar cheese, grated
50 ml / 2 fl oz mayonnaise
50 ml / 2 fl oz natural yoghurt
4 or 5 pickled jalapeño chillies, drained and finely chopped

4 spring onions, finely sliced
juice of $1/2$ lime
pinch sea salt flakes
8 slices of white crusty bread

Mix thoroughly together all the ingredients except the bread in a bowl. Serve in between the slices of bread.

TUNA WITH SWEET AND SOUR CORN

This relish is both sweet and sour at the same time. Make it up and keep in the fridge for up to one week. It is also delicious in hamburgers.

SERVES 4, PREP 15 MINS, COOKING 10 MINS

FOR THE SWEETCORN RELISH
400 g / 14 oz frozen sweetcorn
1 onion, peeled and finely chopped
1/2 red pepper, seeded and finely chopped
4 tbsp white wine vinegar
4 tbsp golden caster sugar

1/2 tsp mustard seeds
sea salt flakes and ground black pepper

200 g / 7 oz tin tuna, in sunflower oil, drained
4 pitta breads
a handful of shredded lettuce

To make the relish, put all the ingredients into a saucepan, bring to the boil, then reduce and simmer for 10 minutes. The mixture should thicken slightly. Allow to cool, cover and leave for at least 1 hour before using. Season the tuna well and divide between the pitta breads. Add a little lettuce to each and spoon in the sweetcorn relish.

TOMATO WITH PESTO TUNA ON TOMATO BREAD

The tomato bread is a good idea if you can get hold of some as it brings out the flavour of the fresh tomatoes. Otherwise choose a moist herb and oil bread.

SERVES 4, PREP 15 MINS

4 ripe plum tomatoes, thinly sliced
8 slices sun-dried tomato bread
2 x 200 g / 7 oz cans tuna in sunflower oil, drained

4 tbsp pesto, see page 151
juice of 1/2 lemon
sea salt flakes and ground black pepper

Arrange the tomato slices on four of the slices of bread. Put the tuna and pesto into a bowl, add the lemon juice and plenty of seasoning and mix together. Scatter the lettuce over the tomatoes, top with the pesto tuna and pop the other slices of bread over the tuna. Serve or wrap up and take away.

FAJITAS WITH SALSA AND GUACAMOLE

You could add chunks of tuna or chicken if you fancy some extra protein.

SERVES 4, PREP 15 MINS, COOKING 5 MINS

8 small flour tortillas

FOR THE SALSA
450 g / 1 lb ripe tomatoes
3 spring onions, finely sliced
1 large green chilli, seeded and finely
chopped
2 tbsp roughly chopped coriander
leaves
juice of 1/2 lemon

FOR THE GUACAMOLE
2 avocados
1 tomato, roughly chopped
1 garlic clove, peeled and crushed
juice of 1/2 lemon
1 tbsp extra virgin olive oil
a few drops Tabasco
2 tbsp chopped coriander leaves

4 tbsp sour cream (optional)

Preheat oven to 200 °C / 400 °F / gas mark 6. Wrap the tortillas in foil and put in the oven for about 5 minutes to warm through.

Meanwhile, to make the salsa, quarter the tomatoes and remove the seeds and core. Cut the flesh into little pieces and put in a bowl with the other salsa ingredients. Mix together well.

To make the guacamole, halve the avocados, remove the stones and peel. Put the avocado flesh and all the other guacamole ingredients, except the coriander, into a food processor and purée until smooth.

Spread the salsa on the tortillas and top with the guacamole. If you want to indulge, a dollop of sour cream could also go on top. Roll up and eat.

SUPER SALADS

Salads are not just about leaves. They are all about having fun with ingredients and flavours in a short space of time. The best salads are a marriage of ingredients that complement one another perfectly, with no single taste overpowering the others.

Salads can be light, perfect with some really fresh crusty bread to mop up the dressing: or they can be chunky, robust affairs that satisfy the emptiest tummy and keep you going until supper! There are salads here for when the cupboard seems bare, such as a rice salad with a simple honey and soy dressing to serve with any fresh vegetables you have to hand. There are splash-out salads, such as duck breast with Chinese dressing, for when you'd like a real treat.

As with all cooking the quality of your ingredients is reflected in the finished result but this is especially the case with salads because you so often eat the vegetables raw or barely cooked. Your ingredients must have flavour and a good texture before you begin – limp vegetables will still be limp in even the nicest of dressings! Whenever possible, buy organic vegetables and salads; the flavour comparisons with other vegetables is often staggering.

These salads are not designed to be followed to the letter, if you want to change quantities or actual ingredients then have fun swapping them around.

Many of these salads travel really well. All you need are a selection of some jazzy plastic containers to pack your salads in.

There can be few things more pleasurable than taking a box of delicious salad to work, on a picnic or wherever else you may be going. Just remember to pack a fork and, if the salad is fish or chicken, keep it in the fridge until you eat. Bon appétit!

Tip: keep the dressing separate until lunchtime. Take the dressing in a little screw-top jar or bottle and drizzle over just before you are ready to eat. This is particularly important with leaf-based salads, keeping the salad crisp rather than letting it go limp.

SWEET POTATO SALAD WITH CHICKEN AND BACON

Sweet potatoes are not in fact, related to potatoes at all. They're a member of the morning glory family. However they look like potatoes, cook like potatoes and are called potatoes. I have made soups with them, griddled them, mashed and roasted them. This was the first salad I ever used them in. New potatoes make a delicious salad, I thought, so why not sweet potatoes? So here it is – a sweet potato salad with chicken and bacon.

SERVES 4, PREP 20 MINS, COOKING 20 MINS

900 g / 2 lb sweet potato, peeled and diced
2 tbsp olive oil
2 skinless chicken breasts
8 rashers bacon
150 g / 5 oz spinach leaves

FOR THE DRESSING
50 ml / 2 fl oz white wine
2 tbsp olive oil
sea salt flakes and ground black pepper

Bring a pan of water to the boil, add the sweet potato and cook until just tender, then drain. Meanwhile, heat half the olive oil in a frying pan, add the chicken and cook for 5 minutes. add the bacon and continue to cook for a further 10 minutes or until both the chicken and bacon is cooked. Slice the chicken into thin strips and snip the bacon with scissors into little pieces. put the chicken and bacon into a bowl. Add the remaining olive oil to the pan and sauté the cooked sweet potato until golden. add to the chicken and bacon.

To make the dressing, deglaze the pan with the wine, add the olive oil and season. Drizzle the dressing over the chicken and potato mixture and toss together well. Leave to cool and serve on top of the spinach leaves.

COUSCOUS SALAD WITH CHICKEN AND APRICOTS

I have used couscous in quite a few recipes in this book and as I have said before, it is easy to use and very quick. The perfect way to have carbohydrate in a hurry.

SERVES 4, PREP 15 MINS, COOKING 25 MINS

2 dtsp olive oil
25 g / 1 oz butter
1 large onion, peeled and sliced
1 tsp cumin seeds, toasted and crushed
2 chicken breasts

1 tsp cayenne pepper, plus extra for dusting
250 g / 9 oz couscous
175 g / 6 oz dried ready-to-eat apricots
50 g / 2 oz mixed herb salad

Heat 15 ml / 1 tbsp of the oil and butter in a large frying pan, add the onion and ground cumin and cook over a medium heat for 5 minutes. Add the chicken breasts skin-side down and cook for 20 minutes, turning halfway through.

Meanwhile, put 225 ml / 9 fl oz water in a saucepan, add the cayenne pepper and remaining oil and heat gently. Add the couscous and stir with a wooden spoon. Cover and remove from the heat for 3 minutes or until the water is absorbed.

Allow the chicken to rest for 5 minutes before slicing into thin strips. Add the apricots and onion mixture to the couscous. Scatter the herbs into containers and spoon over the couscous. Arrange the chicken on top, sprinkle with a little cayenne pepper. Leave to cool and keep in the fridge until needed.

MANGO SALSA WITH CHICKEN BREASTS

For this you need really ripe and fragrant mangoes. To tell if mangoes are ripe, smell the fruit, if you can smell mango they are ready. You can test other fruits for ripeness in this way.

SERVES 4, PREP 15 MINS (PLUS 1 HOUR MARINATING TIME), COOKING 15–20 MINS

FOR THE SALSA
2 ripe mangoes
1/2 red onion, peeled and diced
1/2 red chilli, seeded and sliced
1/2 cucumber, seeded and diced
3 tbsp white wine vinegar

1 dtsp caster sugar
3 tbsp fresh coriander leaves, roughly chopped

4 chicken breasts
oil, for shallow-frying

To make the salsa, peel, halve and stone the mangoes. Cut the flesh into small cubes and place in a bowl. Add the onion, chilli, cucumber, vinegar and sugar. Mix together well, add the coriander, cover and leave to marinate for at least 1 hour.

Preheat the oven to 180 °C / 350 °F / gas mark 4. Fry the chicken breasts, skin-side down for a couple of minutes or until the skin is brown and crispy. Transfer to the oven and cook for 15–20 minutes or until cooked through and the juices run clear. Leave to cool, slice thinly and serve with the salsa.

Warm bacon salad with spinach and Stilton

If you don't like Stilton try one of the milder blue cheeses such as Roquefort or Dolcelatte, or even Cambazola. Also baby spinach is much nicer than the big older leaves. You don't even need to remove the stalks, just wash it really well (although nowadays you can buy it ready washed!). Nut oils are great for making salad dressings, but you don't need a large quantity as they are strongly flavoured.

Serves 4, Prep 15 mins, Cooking 15 mins

8 rashers smoked back bacon
675 g / 1 1/4 lb new potatoes, roughly chopped
1 tbsp walnut oil
1 tbsp olive oil

1 tbsp red wine vinegar
225 g / 8 oz Stilton, cubed
50 g / 2 oz walnuts, roughly chopped
a small bag of fresh spinach leaves, to serve

Heat a large frying pan, add the bacon and cook until crispy. Cook the potatoes in lots of boiling water for about 15 minutes. Drain. Add the potatoes to the bacon, drizzle over the oils and vinegar. Add the Stilton and walnuts and toss everything together well. Serve on the fresh spinach leaves.

STRAWBERRY SALAD WITH BLACK PEPPER

This is a surprisingly delicious combination. Even when you have strawberries for pudding try a quick grind of black pepper over the top, it really enhances their flavour. Strawberries also make a good vinaigrette, especially with something like avocado.

SERVES 4, PREP 15 MINS

175 g / 6 oz strawberries
1/2 cucumber
125 g / 4 oz baby lettuce leaves
50 g / 2 oz walnuts, toasted and
roughly chopped

1 tbsp walnut oil
2 tbsp balsamic vinegar
sea salt flakes and ground black pepper

Hull and quarter the strawberries and place in a bowl. Seed the cucumber and slice into thin strips. Add to the strawberries with the baby lettuce leaves and walnuts. Mix together well. Mix the oil and vinegar in a screw-top jar and shake together well. Drizzle over the salad and season.

GOAT'S CHEESE AND CHICORY SALAD

People generally either love or hate goat's cheese but if you are not a fan substitute a different soft creamy cheese of your choice.

SERVES 4, PREP 15 MINS

FOR THE DRESSING
4 tbsp olive oil
1–2 tbsp Dijon mustard
1 clove garlic, peeled and finely chopped
2 tbsp white or red wine vinegar

125 g / 4 oz chicory leaves
125 g / 4 oz fresh rocket leaves
50 g / 2 oz hazelnuts, toasted and roughly chopped
4 small firm-textured goat's cheeses (approx. 60 g / 2$^{1}/_{2}$ each) OR one 275 g / 10 oz goat's cheese, sliced
crusty bread of your choice

To make the dressing, put all the ingredients in a screw-top jar and shake well. Arrange the chicory and rocket leaves in lunchboxes, add the hazelnuts and toss well. Serve with the dressing, the cheese and crusty bread.

WILD RICE WITH HONEY AND SOY DRESSING

The combination of wild and Basmati rice has got to be my favourite way of eating rice. The soft fluffy Basmati contrasts the nutty wild rice. I love it for its nutty flavour and nutritional value; it contains nine of the essential amino acids and is a good source of fibre. The two require different cooking times, but Tilda have developed a product that combines the two, they have done the hard work for us. The rice in their pack only needs one cooking time.

SERVES 4, PREP 15 MINS, COOKING 20 MINS

300 g / 11 oz Basmati and wild rice
2 tbsp olive oil
2 red onions, peeled and sliced into thin strips
2 carrots, washed
150 g / 5 oz sugar snap peas, halved lengthways

FOR THE DRESSING
2 tbsp white wine vinegar
1 tbsp soy sauce
2 tbsp wholegrain mustard
2 tbsp clear honey
180 ml / 6 fl oz extra virgin olive oil
sea salt flakes and ground black pepper

Three-quarter fill a saucepan with water, bring to the boil. Add the rice, stir and return to the boil, cooking according to instructions on the pack. Drain, rinse and transfer to a bowl. Cut the carrot into thin strips. Heat the oil in a frying pan, add the onions and sauté for 5 minutes, until soft and golden. Add the carrots and sugar snap peas and cook for another few minutes until the vegetables are just cooked, but still crunchy. Leave to cool then add to the rice.

Put all the dressing ingredients in a screw-top jar and shake well. Drizzle over the salad, toss everything together and season.

TUSCAN BREAD SALAD

If you have any stale bread lying around, this salad is for you. Alternatively, use a ciabatta bread as it has a slightly tougher exterior than other breads so it keeps its shape well and the middle part is very good at absorbing the flavours from the dressing.

SERVES 4, PREP 20 MINS, COOKING 15 MINS

3 yellow peppers
1 large stale or ciabatta loaf
750 g / 1 1/2 lb ripe plum tomatoes
1 cucumber

FOR THE DRESSING
2 cloves garlic, peeled and crushed

2 tbsp red wine vinegar
6 tbsp extra virgin olive oil
sea salt flakes and ground black pepper

15 g / 1/2 oz basil leaves, roughly chopped
15 g / 1/2 oz chives, roughly chopped

Preheat the grill to high and grill the peppers until black all over. Seal in a plastic bag and leave to sweat and cool. Remove the skin and cut the flesh into strips. Cut the bread into large bite-size pieces and put in a large bowl. Quarter the tomatoes and remove the seeds. Halve the cucumber lengthways, remove the seeds and cut each half into bite-size pieces. Add to the bread with the tomatoes and pepper strips.

Put all the dressing ingredients in a screw-top jar and shake well. Drizzle over the salad. Scatter the herbs over the top. Leave the salad at room temperature for at least 1 hour before serving drizzled with extra virgin olive oil to taste.

SEAFOOD AND FRESH BASIL SALAD

You can either shell the prawns when you have cooked them or leave them on. I love them with the shell on, it adds a bit of crunch. I am being serious – the shell is really quite tasty.

SERVES 4, PREP 15 MINS, COOKING 5 MINS

5 vine ripened tomatoes
400 g / 14 oz cleaned squid
12 raw prawns, heads removed
12 scallops
2 tbsp olive oil
sea salt flakes and ground black pepper
2 avocados

juice of 2 limes

FOR THE DRESSING
4 tbsp extra virgin olive oil
a large handful of fresh basil
1 clove garlic, peeled and crushed
2 limes, cut into wedges

Pour boiling water over the tomatoes, leave for a maximum 20 seconds, then refresh in cold water, drain and peel. Cut the flesh into little pieces, put in a bowl.
Cut the squid into thick rings, put in another bowl. Place the prawns and scallops in a third bowl. drizzle the oil over both bowls of seafood and season each. Heat a griddle pan until hot and add the prawns and scallops. Cook them for a couple of minutes, then add them to the tomatoes. Place the squid in the pan and cook for just a few seconds. Add to the prawns, scallops and tomatoes. Halve the avocados, remove the stones, peel and slice the flesh into thick chunks, add to the tomato and cooked fish. Mix together the dressing ingredients and pour over the avocado mixture. Season to taste and leave to cool. Pop into containers, keep refrigerated, and serve with lime wedges.

ORANGE AND CARROT SALAD

Use small, sweet, new carrots for a really fresh, delicious salad. When I say small I don't mean baby, which may look lovely but can be somewhat lacking in flavour. If you buy fresh carrots with their green leafy fronds still attached, cut them off quite quickly as they have a tendency to draw the nutrients out of the carrots themselves. All the best flavours and nutrients are in the skin so avoid peeling them. Usually a good scrub will be sufficient.

SERVES 4, PREP 10 MINS, COOKING 5 MINS

450 g / 1 lb carrots, scrubbed and cut into thin matchsticks
125 g / 4 oz pine nuts
4 oranges
100 g / 4 oz raisins

2 tbsp parsley, finely chopped
150 ml / 5 fl oz (1/4 pint) orange juice
1 dtsp wholegrain mustard
2 tbsp extra virgin olive oil
sea salt flakes and ground black pepper

Place the carrots in a large salad bowl. Heat a non-stick frying pan, and dry-fry the pine nuts for about 5 minutes, turning all the time, until lightly browned. Peel and segment the oranges. Mix together the carrots, pine nuts, orange segments, raisins, and parsley. In a small jug, mix together orange juice, mustard, and olive oil. Season to taste, pour over salad and chill until ready to serve.

POTATO AND AVOCADO WITH SOUR CREAM AND MINT DRESSING

Because of the avocado in this recipe, it is best if this salad is kept for only a few hours. If, however, you like the sound of new potatoes with sour cream and mint but you need a more robust salad, leave out the avocado. It will still taste delicious and will keep for much longer.

SERVES 4, PREP 10 MINS, COOKING 15 MINS

800 g / 1 3/4 lb baby new potatoes
sea salt flakes
2 sprigs mint
200 g / 7 oz Feta cheese
2 avocados

juice of 1 lemon
300 ml / 1/2 pt sour cream
a handful of mint leaves, finely chopped
1/2 tsp cayenne pepper

Cut the potatoes into bite-sized pieces and put into a large saucepan with salt and mint sprigs. Bring to the boil and cook for 15 minutes or until tender. Allow to cool. Cut the Feta into 2.5 cm / 1 inch cubes. Skin the avocados, then halve them and remove the stones. Cut the flesh lengthways into wedges and sprinkle with lemon juice. Arrange the potatoes, Feta, and avocado in a shallow bowl or platter. In a separate bowl, mix together the sour cream, chopped mint and cayenne pepper. Drizzle over the salad and chill until ready to serve.

ROASTED AUBERGINE SALAD

Aubergines can be really yummy and meaty. However they can be bland, so you need to add lots of pungent ingredients like black olives, anchovies and tomato purée. If you have time, leave the dish overnight to allow the flavours to develop. For a less salty version, use pine nuts instead of anchovies.

SERVES 4, PREP 15 MINS, COOKING 20 MINS

2 large aubergines
4 tbsp olive oil, plus extra for brushing
sea salt flakes and ground black pepper
4 plum tomatoes
16 black olives, halved and stoned

4 anchovies
1 tbsp tomato purée
1 tsp brown sugar
a handful of fresh basil leaves

Preheat the oven to 200 °C / 400 °F / gas mark 6. Cut aubergine into 2.5 cm /1 in cubes. Place on a baking tray and brush the pieces with olive oil and sprinkle with a little sea salt. Bake for 20 minutes, turning all the time until golden brown and skin is tender. Leave to stand until cool. Cut the tomatoes into eighths and place in a bowl or on a salad platter with the aubergine and olives. Place the anchovies, tomato purée, olive oil and sugar in a food processor and blend until smooth, or grind until smooth with a pestle and mortar. Pour over the aubergines and leave for at least 10 minutes. Top with fresh basil leaves just before serving.

COUSCOUS AND ONION SALAD

Whenever a salad demands large quantities of oil, try to use a really good-quality extra virgin oil. Being a food writer, I have been to Italy to see olive oil being pressed, beginning with the olives being picked from the trees. It was fascinating. Ever since this trip I have used extra virgin olive oil for most things, just because I love its flavour. Carapelli is my favourite.

SERVES 4–6, PREP 30 MINS, COOKING 2 MINS

300 g / 11 oz couscous
1 tbsp mustard seeds
4 pieces of stem ginger, finely diced
2 shallots, peeled and finely sliced
2 red onions, peeled and finely diced

juice and zest of 1 lime
2 garlic cloves, peeled and crushed
25 g / 1 oz parsley, chopped
150 ml / 1/4 pint extra virgin olive oil

Place the couscous in a large bowl and just cover with boiling water. Leave for 10 minutes while the couscous expands and absorbs the water. Fluff up the grains with a fork. Dry-fry the mustard seeds in a frying pan until they begin to pop and swell. Mix all the remaining ingredients into the couscous with the mustard seeds and chill until ready to serve.

ASPARAGUS AND PANCETTA WITH WALNUT AND ORANGE VINAIGRETTE

I have chosen to use pancetta in this recipe but you could just as easily use Parma ham — a salt-cured ham with a delicious flavour. Lemon zest is great in this vinaigrette dressing as well, and other soft-leafed herbs instead of the tarragon.

SERVES 4, PREP 5 MINS, COOKING 5 MINS

550 g / 1 1/4 lb asparagus spears
2 x 70 g / 3 oz packets Italian pancetta
3 tbsp walnut oil
1 tbsp grapeseed oil
1 tsp white wine vinegar

1 shallot, peeled and finely chopped
1 tsp golden caster sugar
zest of 1 orange
1 tbsp chopped tarragon
sea salt flakes and ground black pepper

Bring a saucepan of water to the boil. Trim ends of asparagus, drop into boiling water and cook for 3 minutes. Remove from saucepan and plunge into a bowl of cold water. Leave to cool. Wrap slices of pancetta around the asparagus spears or layer the pancetta and asparagus loosely in a shallow dish. Place the remaining ingredients into a screw-top jar and shake vigorously. Leave the dressing to stand for 20 minutes before pouring over the asparagus.

EGYPTIAN SALAD

This is an idea taken from markets and side stalls around Egypt. Usually called *Koshiri*, it can be as spicy or garlicky as you like and the brave-hearted might like it with extra-hot chilli. It is very often served with meats and boiled eggs. I have kept to the traditional dried lentils, but there are so many quite good canned lentils available nowadays that you could use one of these. Just remember to wash them first to remove the salty water.

SERVES 4–6, PREP 10 MINS, COOKING 15 MINS

250 g / 9 oz lentils vertes (speckled lentils)
sea salt flakes
75 ml / 3 fl oz olive oil
200 g / 7 oz vermicelli noodles
4 garlic cloves, peeled and finely chopped

1 red onion, peeled and finely diced
1 tbsp chilli flakes
2 tbsp tomato purée
4 tomatoes, seeded and diced
1 tsp white wine vinegar

Cover lentils with cold water in a medium saucepan. Bring to the boil and boil rapidly for 10 minutes, then simmer gently for 10 minutes or until tender. Drain and cool. Bring another pan of water to the boil, add a pinch of salt and 1 tbsp of the oil. Crush the vermicelli into small pieces and drop into the boiling water. Cook for about 5 minutes until tender. Heat 2 tbsp of the remaining olive oil in a frying pan and sauté the garlic and onion until golden. Add the chilli flakes, tomato purée and tomatoes. Reduce the heat and mix in vinegar. Leave to cool. Mix together all the lentils and noodles and blend in the dressing. Serve warm or cold.

SCALLOP, MANGO AND SPINACH SALAD

If you cannot find good fresh scallops, substitute prawns. The citrus flavours of lemon grass and lemon in the dressing are perfect for shellfish.

SERVES 4, PREP 5 MINS, COOKING 10 MINS

50 g / 2 oz butter
4 tbsp olive oil
zest of 1/2 lemon
1 stalk of lemon grass
5 mm/ 1/4 in ginger root
450 g / 1 lb scallops
1 mango

150 g / 5 oz spinach leaves, stalks
trimmed
2 tbsp fish sauce (available from all
good supermarkets)
1 tbsp rice vinegar
2 tsp sugar
sea salt flakes and ground black pepper

Melt the butter with the oil in a frying pan. Add lemon zest, lemon grass, and ginger, cook for 1 minute. Toss scallops into pan and cook for 2–3 minutes, turning once. Remove the scallops and cool. Save juices in pan. Peel and halve the mango, remove the stone and cut the flesh into strips. Divide the spinach, mango, and scallops between four plates or lunchboxes. Return the frying pan with the reserved juices back on a low heat. Add fish sauce, rice vinegar and sugar and season to taste. Heat until bubbling for about 2–3 minutes, being careful that it does not brown. Serve hot if you are eating immediately or leave until cold before adding to the salad if you are taking with you in a lunchbox.

PEAR, PEPPER, PECAN AND PECORINO SALAD

Choose sweet ripe pears with a wonderful flavour and soft skin. To check
if pears are ripe, they should 'give' very slightly around the stem, but should
not be squashy. If you cannot find pears with soft skins, you might like to peel
them before adding them to the salad.

SERVES 4, PREP 15 MINS, COOKING 50 MINS

2 red peppers
2 yellow peppers
2 tbsp extra virgin olive oil
125 g / 4 oz pecan nuts

4 pears
juice of $1/2$ lemon
50 g / 2 oz Pecorino cheese shavings
ground black pepper

Preheat oven to 200 °C / 400 °F / gas mark 6. Put the red and yellow peppers
on a baking tray and roast for 30 minutes until their skins are black and the
flesh is soft. Remove from the oven, seal in a plastic bag and leave to sweat and
cool. Peel away the skins. Halve and seed the peppers, then cut the flesh into
strips. Place in a bowl and cover with the olive oil. Roughly chop the pecans
and dry-fry until they start to brown (this really brings out their flavour). Peel
and core the pears, slice thickly and toss in the lemon juice. Arrange the pears,
peppers, and pecans in a dish and top with Pecorino shavings. Drizzle over oil
from the peppers and season with ground black pepper.

BEEF AND BEETROOT SALAD

This is delicious with roasted red onions and baked potatoes for a more substantial lunch. To help make this salad quickly, I have used cooked beetroot, however remember to choose cooked beetroot that has not been steeped in vinegar.

SERVES 4, PREP 15 MINS, COOKING 10 MINS (APPROX.)

1-2 tbsp oil
2 fillet steaks, trimmed of fat
sea salt flakes and ground black pepper
250 g / 9 oz cooked beetroot, thickly sliced
1 bunch of watercress, washed and picked over

FOR THE DRESSING
1 tbsp red wine vinegar
1 tbsp water
1 dtsp creamed horseradish
1 tbsp olive oil

Heat a heavy-based frying pan over a high heat and add the oil. Rub the steaks with salt and pepper and fry on each side for a few minutes, depending on the thickness of the steak and your preference. (As a guide, for a medium-rare steak, fry for 5 minutes on one side and 3–5 minutes on the other side.) Remove the steaks from the pan and leave to rest for 10 minutes then slice thinly.

To make the dressing, deglaze the pan with the vinegar and water. Pour the liquid into a screw-top jar, add the rest of the dressing ingredients, shake and season.

Arrange the beef and beetroot slices over the watercress and serve with the dressing.

FIELD AND BUTTON MUSHROOMS WITH BACON, GARLIC AND ALMONDS

In this recipe, I have roasted the garlic for a little before adding it to the oil to give it a slightly sweeter and milder flavour. Field mushrooms are so thick and meaty they have a wonderful flavour and texture. I often just fry them in a little butter, scatter over lots of herbs and serve them on toast.

SERVES 4, PREP 15 MINS (PLUS INFUSING TIME), COOKING 20 MINS

4 large field mushrooms, wiped and thickly sliced
150 g / 5 oz button mushrooms, cleaned
8 garlic cloves, peeled
100 ml / 3½ fl oz olive oil

ground black pepper
8 rashers of bacon
50 g / 2 oz flaked almonds
1 lollo bianco lettuce, washed
2 tbsp snipped chives

Preheat the oven to 200 °C / 400 °F / gas mark 6. Put both types of mushrooms in a roasting tray with the whole garlic cloves. Drizzle with a little of the olive oil, season with black pepper and bake in the oven for 15 minutes. Remove and leave to cool. Grill the bacon, or cook in the oven, until crisp. Allow to cool and cut into thin strip. Dry-fry the flaked almonds in a frying pan until lightly browned. Leave to cool.

Shake the baked garlic cloves well in a screw-top jar with the remaining oil, then leave to infuse for at least 20 minutes. Put the lettuce leaves on plates or in lunchboxes. Arrange the mushrooms and bacon over the lettuce leaves. Sprinkle over the almonds and fresh chives. Dress with the garlic oil.

ROASTED MEDITERRANEAN VEGETABLES

These roasted vegetables are also excellent mixed with some pasta or sand-wiched between two thick slices of ciabatta. If you have any leftover meat such as chicken or beef, add a few slices, mix everything together and serve with a little grainy mustard. Vegetarians may also like to add a little tapenade to the salad instead.

SERVES 4, PREP 15 MINS, COOKING 40–45 MINS

1 red pepper, seeded and sliced into 1/2 cm strips
1 yellow pepper, seeded and sliced into 1/2 cm strips
1 red onion, skinned and cut into thin wedges
1 small fennel bulb, trimmed and cut into eighths
2 courgettes, diagonally cut into ovals

2 plum tomatoes, halved
4 garlic cloves, peeled
sprigs of herbs, such as rosemary or thyme
sea salt flakes and ground black pepper
2 tbsp olive oil
a handful of flat leaf parsley
1 lemon, cut into wedges

Preheat oven to 200 °C / 400 °F / gas mark 6. Put all the prepared vegetables into a large roasting pan with the sprigs of herbs, sprinkle with sea salt and drizzle liberally with olive oil. Mix well – using your hands is easiest! Roast in the oven for 40–45 minutes. Remove and leave to cool. Season again and scatter the parsley over. Serve with lemon wedges for squeezing over the top.

QUICK HUMUS WITH CRUDITÉS

You might think this is more of a quick nibble than a salad, but I've included it here because I find it so easy to eat a big lunchbox full of vegetables with humus for a main meal rather than a snack. Anyway, enjoy it whenever or however you wish to eat it. If you like something with a bit more kick, stir in some paprika and a handful of freshly chopped coriander leaves after you have blended the ingredients together. Humus is also very good in a sandwich with tuna, really ripe plum tomatoes and a little lettuce.

SERVES 4, PREP 10 MINS

400 g / 14 oz can chick peas
2 cloves garlic, peeled
2 tbsp olive oil
juice of 1/2 lemon
1 tsp tahini
sea salt flakes and ground black pepper
baby lettuce leaves

a selection of fresh and tasty vegetables such as carrots, cauliflower, black olives, courgettes, celery, radishes, baby sweet corn prepared as necessary and cut into matchsticks or bite-sized pieces.

Put all the ingredients except the lettuce and vegetables in a food processor and whiz until smooth, or purée for a little less time if you prefer the humus to have a little more texture. Put baby lettuce leaves into lunchboxes, top with the humus and pile vegetables alongside.

PASTA WITH ROASTED RED PEPPERS AND SEARED TUNA

I often grill or roast peppers for salads, sandwiches, purées etc. But to save time, I sometimes roast quite a few together and, once peeled, I keep the flesh in jars with olive oil to use as and when needed. You could also add capers, black olives or cucumber to this salad.

SERVES 4, PREP 15 MINS, COOKING 10 MINS (APPROX.)

2 fresh tuna steaks
4 tbsp olive oil
juice of 1 large lemon
sea salt flakes and ground black pepper

2 red peppers
275 g / 10 oz pasta
a handful of fresh flat leaf parsley, roughly chopped

Put the tuna in a bowl with half of the olive oil, half of the lemon juice and season well. Quarter and seed the peppers, rub them with a little olive oil and place on a baking tray under a very hot grill. Cook until the skins are really blackened, then seal them in a plastic bag and leave to sweat and cool. Peel away the skin and slice the pepper flesh. Cook the pasta until *al dente*, drain and run under cold water. Season well. Heat the remaining olive oil in a heavy-based frying pan and cook the tuna steak for a few minutes on each side (the exact time will depend on the size of the steaks.) Remove from the pan and leave to cool. Deglaze the pan with the remaining lemon juice and pour the juices over the pasta. Slice the cooled tuna thinly, lay on top of the pasta and scatter the parsley over. Pack in a lunchbox or eat immediately.

POTATO AND SMOKED MACKEREL SALAD

This salad also tastes delicious made with smoked salmon instead of smoked mackerel.

SERVES 4, PREP 10 MINS, COOKING 15 MINS

juice of 1 lemon
1 tbsp sunflower oil
1 tsp creamed horseradish
sea salt flakes and ground black pepper

450 g / 1 lb tiny waxy new potatoes
2 smoked mackerel fillets
1 bunch of chives, finely snipped

Mix together the lemon juice, oil and horseradish and season well. Bring a pan of water to the boil, add the potatoes and simmer until cooked (they should be tender when pierced with a knife). Drain and slice. Flake the fish, keeping the flakes as big as possible. Add the fish to the potatoes and drizzle over the dressing while potatoes are still warm, it will absorb the flavours from the oil and lemon. Sprinkle the chives over and eat straight away or allow to cool before packing into containers. Keep refrigerated.

ROASTED SWEET POTATOES WITH CHICKEN SALAD

To make *meaty* satisfying salads, very often you just need to use ingredients that you would use for a normal supper. This salad is an excellent example.

SERVES 4, PREP 15 MINS, COOKING 30 MINS

3 large sweet potatoes, peeled and roughly chopped
4 tbsp extra virgin olive oil
2 skinless boneless chicken breasts

2 cloves garlic, peeled and crushed
1 tbsp lime juice
a handful of flat leaf parsley
sea salt flakes and ground black pepper

Preheat the oven to 200 °C / 400 °F / gas mark 6. Put the potatoes on a baking sheet, drizzle with half of the oil and roast for 15 minutes. Add the chicken breasts to the pan and roast for another 15 minutes. Leave to stand for 15 minutes, then slice the chicken. In a separate bowl, mix together the garlic, lime juice, parsley and remaining oil. Season and drizzle over the potatoes. Serve immediately or leave to cool and pack into lunchboxes.

CARAMELISED ONIONS, CHICK PEAS, FETA AND MINT

Caramelised onions are just amazing. They are so versatile: use them to make pizzas with Mozzarella, squidge them into sandwiches with cold meats or toss them through risottos. There are many ways of caramelising onions but if you are short of time you can encourage their own natural sugars to turn to caramel by adding a few teaspoonsfuls of soft brown sugar. Salads like this one travel really well.

SERVES 4, PREP 10 MINS, COOKING 20 MINS

3 tbsp olive oil
1 red chilli, seeded and diced
2 red onions, peeled and sliced
4 cloves garlic, peeled and crushed
2 tsp soft brown sugar
75 ml / 3 fl oz red wine vinegar

200 g / 7 oz Feta cheese, crumbled
2 x 400 g / 14 oz cans chick peas, drained
a handful of fresh mint leaves
sea salt flakes and ground black pepper

Heat the oil in a saucepan. Add the chilli, onions, garlic and sugar and cook very gently for 15 minutes, stirring frequently to prevent the onions from sticking. Add the vinegar, bring to the boil and cook for about 2 minutes until the vinegar has evaporated. Add all of the remaining ingredients, mix well and leave to stand for 15 minutes. Season and serve or chill until needed.

JAPANESE-STYLE TUNA SALAD WITH WASABI SAUCE

I have added yoghurt and lemon juice to the wasabi (Japanese horseradish) paste to make a mild dressing, you may prefer to do as they do in Japan and serve straight wasabi (beware, it is extremely hot).

SERVES 4, PREP 15 MINS, COOKING 10 MINS

FOR THE MARINADE
2 tbsp saké
2 tbsp soy sauce
1 tbsp chilli oil
juice of 1/2 lemon
1 tbsp vegetable oil

4 x 175g / 5 oz tuna steaks

FOR THE CUCUMBER SALSA
1 cucumber

1 red onion, peeled
1 tsp sugar
1 tbsp hot water
juice of 1/2 lemon
2 tbsp rice wine vinegar
1 red chilli, seeded and thinly sliced

FOR THE WASABI SAUCE
2 tsp wasabi paste
90 ml / 3 fl oz natural yoghurt
juice of 1/2 lemon

To make the marinade, place all the ingredients in a bowl and mix together well. Add the tuna, cover and refrigerate for at least 4 hours. Heat a griddle pan and cook the tuna steaks for 4 minutes on each side, or until just opaque in the centre. Leave to cool and slice.

To make the salsa; halve the cucumber lengthways and remove the seeds with a spoon. Cut each half into thirds, then thinly slice. Cut the red onion into thin wedges. To make the dressing, dissolve the sugar in the hot water, add the lemon juice and rice wine vinegar and mix together well. In a small bowl, mix together the cucumber, red onion and red chilli. Add the dressing and toss all the ingredients together.

To make the wasabi sauce, mix together all the ingredients. Serve the tuna slices on a pile of the cucumber salsa with a dollop of the wasabi sauce on top.

HOT AND SPICY VEGETABLE SALAD

Noodles with lots of thinly sliced vegetables tossed in a dressing of sesame oil and chilli. Just delicious! Make it for supper, eat it hot and save some for the next day's lunch. Two meals from one session with the wok – lovely.

SERVES 4, PREP 10 MINS, COOKING 5 MINS

1 tbsp oil
2 carrots, trimmed and cut into matchsticks
1 courgette, trimmed and cut into matchsticks
2 sticks of celery, trimmed and cut into matchsticks
50 g / 2 oz mangetout, topped and tailed
1 small red pepper, seeded and thinly sliced
1 small red onion, peeled and thinly sliced

125 g / 4 oz Chinese cabbage (or pak choi), roughly shredded
225 g / 8 oz noodles

FOR THE DRESSING
1 tbsp sesame oil
1 dried red chilli, crushed
1 tsp caster sugar
1 tbsp lime juice
sea salt flakes and ground black pepper

a handful of chopped parsley, to garnish

Heat the oil in a wok, add the vegetables and stir-fry for about 3 minutes until they are just beginning to wilt. Remove from the heat. Cook the noodles according to the packet instructions. Meanwhile, to make the dressing, put all the ingredients in a screw-top jar, seasoning to taste. Strain the cooked noodles and toss with the vegetables and dressing. Scatter the parsley over the top and serve or leave to cool, pack into lunchboxes and chill until needed.

SPICE-CRUSTED CHICKEN SALAD

Whenever possible I use whole spices rather than ground. The important thing to remember is to dry-fry them for a few minutes, then grind them for a really good strong flavour.

SERVES 4, PREP 10 MINS, COOKING 20 MINS

2 tsp coriander seeds, crushed
1 tsp mustard seeds
2 tsp ground paprika
1 tbsp wholegrain mustard
1 tbsp fresh coriander, roughly chopped
1 clove garlic, peeled
zest of 2 oranges

sea salt flakes and ground black pepper
4 boneless skinless chicken breasts
5 tbsp olive oil
200 g / 7 oz sugar snap peas
125 g / 4 oz continental salad
a handful of coriander leaves, roughly chopped

Put the coriander and mustard seeds into a small frying pan and dry-fry for about 2 minutes until the seeds pop. Purée the toasted seeds, paprika, mustard, coriander leaves, garlic and orange zest and a little salt in a food processor or pound in a pestle and mortar. Lay the chicken breasts on a piece of greaseproof paper and spread with the paste, cover with cling film and beat with a rolling pin until flattened. Transfer to a larger shallow heatproof dish and drizzle with 2 tbsp of the olive oil. Cook under a moderate grill for about 20 minutes until golden and cooked through. Cook the sugar snap peas in boiling water for 1 minute, drain and allow to cool. Toss with the salad and the remaining olive oil and season. Slice the chicken and place on the salad. Spoon the cooking juices over and garnish with coriander leaves.

BROAD BEAN, CHILLI AND PANCETTA SALAD

It may seem a hassle, but you do need to take the outer shell off each bean or you will find that they are really tough and not at all pleasant.

SERVES 4, PREP 10 MINS, COOKING 10 MINS

50 ml / 2 fl oz extra virgin olive oil
150 g / 5 oz pancetta
700 g / 1 1/2 lbs fresh hulled or thawed frozen broad beans
1 red chilli, seeded and finely chopped
1 red onion, peeled and finely sliced

2 cloves garlic, peeled and crushed
a handful of fresh mint and tarragon leaves, roughly chopped
1 tbsp red wine vinegar
small pot crème fraîche

Heat the oil in a frying pan, add the pancetta, and cook for 5 minutes until crisp. Add the beans and chilli and sauté for a few seconds. Add the onion and garlic and cook for 1 minute, stirring constantly. Remove from the heat and add the mint, tarragon and vinegar. Leave to cool, then spoon into lunchboxes. Take the crème fraîche with you and serve the salad with a dollop on top.

JAPANESE POTATO SALAD

This is a classic example of an incredibly tasty salad that will not leave you hungry, although if you do like to have a little protein for lunch, simply add some tiger or small prawns – but remember to keep the salad chilled.

SERVES 4, PREP 15 MINS (PLUS STANDING TIME), COOKING 15 MINS

FOR THE DRESSING
1 clove garlic, peeled and finely minced
2 tbsp fresh ginger, peeled and grated
3 tbsp smooth unsalted peanut butter
2 tbsp soy sauce
4 tbsp oyster sauce
50 ml / 2 fl oz rice wine or white wine vinegar

3 tbsp water
sea salt flakes and ground black pepper

850 g / 1 1/4 lb small new potatoes
8 radishes, quartered
25 g / 1 oz watercress

To make the dressing, whisk together all the ingredients until well combined. If the dressing seems too thick, add a little extra water. Leave to stand for 30 minutes before using.

   Cook the potatoes in boiling salted water. Drain. Add the radishes and watercress and mix together. Pop in a container, drizzle over the dressing and it's ready to go. This keeps really well in the fridge for up to 3 days.

PASTA WITH ARTICHOKES, MUSHROOMS AND PESTO

Fresh pesto is almost always far superior to any in a jar. It is really worth the effort and if you use a food processor you can save some time. You can also use rocket instead of basil for a more peppery taste. Make double and keep any left over in a screw-top jar in the fridge for up to 2 weeks. Roasted artichokes are available in jars or from delis.

SERVES 4, PREP 10 MINS, COOKING 15 MINS

350 g / 12 oz dried pasta
1 tbsp olive oil
125 g / 4 oz button mushrooms, washed and halved
75 g / 3 oz roasted artichokes, sliced
125 g / 4 oz cherry tomatoes or baby plum tomatoes, washed and halved
sea salt flakes and ground black pepper

FOR THE PESTO
15 g / 1/2 oz pine nuts, toasted
1 garlic clove, peeled and crushed
sea salt flakes and ground black pepper
75 g / 3 oz basil leaves
8 tbsp extra virgin olive oil
25 g / 1 oz freshly grated Parmesan cheese

Cook the pasta according to the packet instructions. Drain and refresh with cold water. Leave to cool. Heat the olive oil in a saucepan over a high heat and fry the mushroom quickly, stirring often until they are golden brown. Pour into a large bowl with the oil. Add the artichokes and the halved tomatoes and season to taste. To make the pesto, put the pine nuts, garlic, and a pinch of salt and basil into a food processor and whiz to a paste. Gradually add the oil and whizz again until smooth. Stir in the Parmesan. Spoon the pesto into the pasta and toss everything together.

ASPARAGUS WITH SHAVED PARMESAN AND ROCKET SALAD

This is a really light lunch that is perfect if you have a chance to go home for a few minutes. Alternatively, make it up, take to work and enjoy it there, pretending that you are at home with your feet up. Serve with crusty bread.

SERVES 4, PREP 10 MINS, COOKING 10 MINS

450 g / 1 lb asparagus
225 g / 8 oz fresh rocket
75 ml / 3 fl oz olive oil
1 tsp balsamic vinegar

juice 1/2 lemon
sea salt flakes and ground black pepper
125 g / 4 oz fresh Parmesan cheese

Trim the asparagus bottoms by bending them near the bottom – they will snap exactly where the tough part of the stalk ends. Bring a large pan of water to the boil and simmer the asparagus for a few minutes until cooked but still with a bite. Drain. Cut the spears into small pieces and place in a bowl. Add the rocket. Mix together the olive oil, balsamic vinegar, lemon juice and seasoning. Pour over the asparagus and rocket and mix well. Scatter Parmesan cheese over the top, serve or pack into lunchboxes.

ASPARAGUS WITH TOASTED CASHEW NUTS AND ORIENTAL DRESSING

This would also be really delicious with chicken that has been roasted with a lemon and some garlic in the cavity. And with new potatoes this would make a wonderful summer lunch. Make sure you choose a good make when you pick a bottle of soy sauce – Kikkoman is excellent. As a general guide, use light soy sauce with subtle flavours like asparagus and seafood and dark with chicken and red meat.

SERVES 4, PREP 10 MINS, COOKING 10 MINS (APPROX.)

450 g / 1 lb asparagus
1 tsp sesame oil
2 dtsp sunflower oil
1 dtsp light soy sauce
1 dtsp lemon juice

2.5 cm / 1 in piece of root ginger,
peeled and crushed
ground black pepper
50 g / 2 oz cashew nuts, toasted and
chopped

Trim the asparagus bottoms: bend them near the bottom – they will snap exactly where the tough part of the stalk ends. Bring a large pan of water to the boil and cook the asparagus until just done. Mix together the oils, soy sauce, lemon juice, ginger and pepper. Scatter the cashew nuts over the warm asparagus and then drizzle over the dressing. Eat warm or leave to cool and eat later.

ROASTED AUBERGINE, TOMATO SALSA AND TABBOULEH

This is also good with humus (see page 140, or buy a pot from a supermarket). Roasted aubergines and other vegetables are also available from supermarket deli counters.

SERVES 4, PREP 15 MINS

FOR THE SALSA
4 ripe plum tomatoes
25 g / 1 oz sun-dried tomatoes
1/2 red onion
juice of 1 lime
1 fresh mild chilli, seeded and very finely chopped
2 tbsp olive oil
sea salt flakes and ground black pepper

FOR THE TABBOULEH
275 g / 10 oz cracked bulghur wheat
1/2 cucumber
a handful of mint leaves, roughly chopped

200 g / 7 oz chargrilled aubergine (see page 49)

To make the salsa, pour boiling water over the plum tomatoes. Leave for 1 minute, then refresh under cold water. Slip the skins off. On a board over a bowl, to catch the juice, chop the tomato flesh into small chunks. Slice the sun-dried tomatoes into thin slivers and add to the tomatoes. Peel and chop the red onion very finely, add half of the lime juice, chilli, olive oil and seasoning. Mix well and set aside.

   Pour just enough boiling water over the bulghur grains to cover. Cover and set aside until the water is absorbed then fluff up with a fork. Peel and seed the cucumber and chop the flesh into small chunks. Add the cucumber, the remaining lime juice and mint to the bulghur. Stir well and season to taste. Serve the aubergines with the salsa and tabbouleh.

ROASTED AUBERGINE, WITH MOZZARELLA, TOMATO, AND BASIL

I must confess this is delicious served warm straight from the oven. However, if you find that you eat half for supper and have some left over, keep it in the fridge and take it with you the next day for lunch with some crusty bread. You will not be disappointed.

SERVES 4, PREP 20 MINS, COOKING 45 MINS

1 large aubergine
3 tbsp olive oil
sea salt flakes and ground black pepper
3 ripe and red beef tomatoes

200 g / 7 oz Mozzarella cheese
juice of 1/2 lemon
a handful fresh basil, roughly torn

Preheat oven to 200 °C / 400 °F / gas mark 6. Slice the aubergine into rounds 1 cm / 1/2 in thick and place on a baking tray. Drizzle over 2 tbsp olive oil and sprinkle with a little salt. Roast in the oven for 45 minutes. Leave to cool slightly. Add the tomatoes and mozzarella slices to the aubergine. Toss everything together while still warm. Mix the lemon juice with the remaining olive oil and pour over the salad. Scatter the torn basil leaves over. This is even better left a while as the juice seeps out of the tomatoes and you can then use crusty bread to mop up the juices!

A LEAFY GREEN SALAD WITH A FRUITY DRESSING

I have written this recipe just to prove that leafy green salads need not be dull. There are amazing combinations of colour, texture and flavour in the leaves. I have chosen leaves that are quite easy to get hold of but nowadays most supermarkets have such a good choice of mixed bags of leaves that you could just as easily use one of these. This fruity and light dressing is one of my all-time favourites. The chunky Pecorino croûtons add crunch and flavour. You can also jazz up salads by adding bits of crispy bacon, nuts, roasted onion slices or thinly crisp apple slices.

SERVES 4, PREP 15 MINS

125 g / 4 oz mache
125 g / 4 oz frisée leaves
125 g / 4 oz lollo rosso

FOR THE DRESSING
3 tbsp orange juice

1 tbsp raspberry vinegar
sea salt flakes and ground black pepper

Croûtons (see page 161) tossed in
grated Pecorino cheese, to serve

Roughly tear the leaves and mix together in a bowl. Shake together all of the dressing ingredients in a screw-top jar and pour over the salad. Scatter the crunchy croûtons, together with the grated Pecorino cheese over the top and serve.

GUACAMOLE

Avocados are not brilliant in lunchboxes as they have a tendency to go brown. They are best taken whole, then halved and eaten at lunchtime with a pre-prepared dressing or a squeeze of lemon and some salt and pepper. A little crisp bacon on the top is nice too. If you are going to take avocados in your lunchbox, the most successful idea is to mash them up with a few other delicious ingredients and turn them into a guacamole. Just make sure that the surface is covered with cling film and it will be perfect at lunchtime. It's delicious served with corn or tortilla chips. This is also a perfect accompaniment to the spicy Mexican bean salad (see page 158).

SERVES 4, PREP 15 MINS

2 ripe avocados
juice of 1/2 lemon
1 tsp Tabasco sauce
1 small garlic clove, peeled and crushed

1 tbsp olive oil
sea salt and ground black pepper
1 large, ripe tomato
1/2 red onion, peeled and very finely chopped

Peel the avocados and put the flesh into a bowl. Add the lemon juice, Tabasco, garlic, oil and some salt and pepper. Mash with a fork. Cover the tomato with boiling water and leave for 1 minute. Slip off the skin and chop the flesh finely. Add the onion and the tomato to the avocado mixture. Mix well and season to taste.

   If you prefer a really smooth guacamole, put all the ingredients in a food processor and whiz for a few seconds until smooth. Keep covered and refrigerated.

SPICY MEXICAN BEAN SALAD

This is really yummy with corn chips and guacamole (see page 157). It's a good filling for a jacket potato or an accompaniment to grilled chicken. Canned kidney beans are fine. It's an incredibly quick salad and nice with any kind of cheese or onion bread.

SERVES 4, PREP 15 MINS

400 g / 14 oz can kidney beans, drained
2 spring onions, cleaned and finely chopped
1/2 red onion peeled and thinly sliced
200 g / 7 oz can sweetcorn, drained
1 fresh red chilli, seeded and finely chopped

1 red pepper, seeded and thinly sliced
225 g / 8 oz cherry tomatoes, quartered
juice of 1 lime
4 tbsp olive oil
a large handful of fresh coriander, roughly chopped
sea salt flakes and ground black pepper

In a large bowl combine the beans, spring onions, red onion, sweetcorn, chilli, red pepper and cherry tomatoes. Mix together the lime juice, olive oil and coriander leaves. Pour over the salad and mix everything gently together. Leave for 1 hour before eating so that the flavours develop.

CHUNKY GREEK SALAD

You could use Halloumi cheese instead of Feta, if you prefer. Remember that Feta is quite salty, so you will probably only need freshly ground black pepper for the seasoning. Leave the salad at room temperature before you eat it to allow the flavours to develop. I adore the elegantly almond-shaped Calamata olives and the smaller ones often have the richest flavour. But you can choose any olives that you really like; if possible go to a deli and taste a few types before you buy them.

SERVES 4, PREP 15 MINS

225 g / 8 oz Feta cheese, cut into
1 cm / $^1/_2$ in cubes
1 cucumber, peeled, seeded and cut into chunks
6 ripe plum tomatoes, cut into wedges
1 small red onion, peeled, halved and thinly sliced

75 g / 3 oz Greek or Calamata olives
1 small garlic clove, crushed
1 sprig of fresh thyme
juice of $^1/_2$ lemon
5 tbsp virgin olive oil
2 tbsp white wine vinegar
ground black pepper

In a large bowl toss together the Feta, cucumber, tomatoes, onion and olives. Mix together the garlic, thyme, lemon juice, olive oil, vinegar and pepper in a small bowl. Pour over the salad. This salad is best served at room temperature.

REFRESHING FENNEL SALAD

Fennel can be eaten raw or cooked, but one of my favourite ways of eating it is griddled with thin shavings of Parmesan scattered over the top. This is also delicious with toasted sunflower seeds or pumpkin seeds sprinkled over.

SERVES 4, PREP 20 MINS

175 g / 6 oz Feta cheese
1 large red onion, peeled and thinly sliced
1 cucumber, peeled, cored and sliced
1 head of fennel, washed and very thinly sliced

75 g / 3 oz black olives
4 large oranges
4 tbsp olive oil
2 tbsp parsley, roughly chopped
sea salt flakes and ground black pepper

In a large bowl gently combine the Feta, onion, cucumber, fennel and olives. Use a very sharp knife to cut away the skin of the oranges following the curve of the orange, catching all the juice in a bowl below your chopping board. Make sure you remove all the bitter white pith. Then, working round the orange, cut it into segments, cutting between the membranes towards the centre of each orange and removing any pips as you go. This may seem fiddly but it is really worth the effort as the salad is then so easy to eat. Separate the orange segments from the juice, add them to the salad and mix together gently. Mix together the olive oil, 90 ml / 6 tbsp of the orange juice and the parsley and season to taste. Pour over the salad and leave to marinade for at least 1 hour before eating.

Classic Caesar Salad

Caesar salad is a classic mixture. The lettuce should be really crisp, the dressing pungent and the croûtons crunchy. You must have really good fresh Parmesan cheese and fresh eggs. You don't need to add salt to the dressing as anchovies are quite salty.

Serves 4, Prep 20 mins

2 fresh cos lettuces

FOR THE CROÛTONS
4 slices of good quality white bread, crusts removed
sunflower oil, for shallow-frying

FOR THE DRESSING
1 free-range egg
2 anchovy fillets
1 large clove garlic, peeled and crushed
1 tsp mustard powder
1 tsp Worcestershire sauce
juice of 1/2 lemon
ground black pepper
5 fl oz / 1/4 pt olive oil
2 tbsp freshly grated Parmesan

2 oz Parmesan shavings

Arrange lettuce in a bowl, tearing the larger leaves as you go. To make the croûtons, cut the bread into small cubes. Heat some oil in a heavy-based frying pan until a single cube of bread fizzles in it. Fry the bread cubes, turning constantly. Keep an eye on them as they will turn brown quickly. Drain on kitchen paper. To make the dressing, put the egg into a food processor with the anchovies, garlic, mustard, Worcestershire sauce, lemon juice and black pepper. Gradually add the oil while the machine is running. When it has all been incorporated add the grated Parmesan and give it one quick whiz. The dressing should have the same consistency as cream. When you are ready to eat, pour over the dressing and garnish with the croûtons and Parmesan.

BUTTER-BEAN SALAD

This would be really nice served with tuna fish. Bonita tuna is available from delis and specialist food shops. It's a bit pricier than your average tuna, but you really should try it at least once – it's delicious. Otherwise a good tuna in sunflower oil is fine.

SERVES 4, PREP 15 MINS, COOKING 5 MINS

350 g / 12 oz cooked butter-beans
25 g / 1 oz unsalted butter
1 small clove of garlic, peeled and crushed
2 leeks, washed and very finely sliced
a handful of flat leaf parsley, roughly chopped

a handful of coriander leaves, roughly chopped
2 tbsp olive oil
juice of 1 lemon
sea salt flakes and ground black pepper

Put the butter-beans into a large bowl. Heat the butter in a saucepan, add the garlic and cook it until it is just turning brown – any more and it will taste bitter. Add the leeks and fry them for 2 minutes, stirring constantly. (They should still be a little crunchy.) Add the parsley and coriander and stir well. Tip everything into the bowl with the butter-beans. Mix together the olive oil, lemon juice and seasoning and pour over the beans. This is nice served while the leeks are still warm, but if you can leave it overnight the flavours really develop.

Morrocan chick pea salad

This is nice with cold cooked chicken or tuna mixed in with it and a salad of spinach leaves. It's very easy to transport – just pop it into a box and go.

SERVES 4, PREP 40 MINS (PLUS 1 HOUR CHILLING TIME), COOKING 6 MINS

450 g / 1 lb cooked chick peas
4 tbsp olive oil
1 large red onion, peeled and chopped
2 garlic cloves, peeled and crushed
1/2 tsp cumin
1 tsp mild curry powder
1 tsp chilli powder
1/2 tsp paprika
1 red pepper, seeded and finely chopped

a handful of roughly chopped flat leaf parsley
juice of 1/2 lemon
sea salt flakes and ground black pepper

FOR THE YOGHURT SAUCE
300 g / 11 oz Greek yoghurt
1 small clove of garlic, peeled and crushed
a pinch of paprika

Put the chick peas into a large bowl. In a frying pan heat 15 ml / 1 tbsp of the oil. Add the onion and garlic and cook gently for 5 minutes until the onion is soft and translucent. Add the cumin, curry powder, chilli powder and paprika. Cook, stirring constantly, for 1 minute. Using a spatula, scrape everything out into the bowl with the chick peas and stir well. Add the chopped pepper to the salad with the parsley, lemon juice and remaining olive oil. Season, stir gently and leave to marinate for at least 1 hour.

To make the yoghurt sauce, mix together the yoghurt and garlic and season to taste. Dust with a little paprika. Serve with the chick pea salad.

CORONATION CHICKEN SALAD

This is a fantastic way of using up leftover cooked chicken. It's also good served with cold Basmati rice; try tossing the rice with a little olive oil, finely grated lemon rind, and finely chopped parsley or coriander. Make sure that when you use cold rice it is kept well refrigerated and never reheated – badly kept cooked rice is one of the most common causes of food poisoning.

SERVES 4, PREP 15 MINS

4 cooked chicken breasts or
350 g /12 oz cooked chicken
1 tbsp mild curry powder
2 tbsp lime juice
1 dtsp mango chutney
8 tbsp good quality mayonnaise
140 ml / ¼ pint whipped cream or
fromage frais

sea salt flakes and ground black pepper
1 ripe mango
125 g / 4 oz black grapes
1 tbsp coriander or parsley, roughly
chopped

Shred the chicken into a large bowl. In a separate bowl, mix together the curry powder, lime juice and chutney. Add the mayonnaise and mix well, then gently fold in the cream or fromage frais and season. Cut the mango flesh either side of the stone, skin, and then cut the flesh into bite-sized pieces. Wash and dry the grapes, then halve them and remove the pips. Add to the chicken with the mango. Carefully mix the sauce into the chicken and sprinkle the herbs over the top. Put into lunchboxes and keep refrigerated.

COLESLAW

This is a yummy classic – delicious in sandwiches with ham and also really good in baked potatoes for supper. There are all kinds of ingredients you can add to this basic recipe, such as raisins or even toasted sunflower seeds. Just see how you feel. For a delicious variation that is particularly good with turkey, try using red cabbage, red onion and a handful of dried cranberries. Coleslaw is best eaten within a day of being made.

SERVES 4, PREP 15 MINS

1 medium green cabbage
4 carrots
1/2 onion, peeled
200 g / 7 oz good quality mayonnaise

juice of 1/2 lemon
1 tsp sugar
sea salt flakes and ground black pepper
1 tbsp fresh parsley, finely chopped

Discard the outer leaves and cut the cabbage into quarters. Remove the tough core and finely slice each chunk. Put into a large bowl with the carrots and onion. Mix together the mayonnaise, lemon juice and sugar and season to taste. Mix into the vegetables and stir in the parsley. Cover and refrigerate until needed.

POTATO SALAD WITH A HERB DRESSING

Potato salad is really versatile – it doesn't have to be a big soggy mass drowning in mayonnaise. Adding a fresh herb dressing to warm potatoes means they really take up the flavour and are quite delicious. There are lots of things you can add – toasted walnuts, crumbled Stilton or Roquefort, or cooked sliced sausages, especially some of the speciality ones.

SERVES 4, PREP 20 MINS (PLUS 5 MINS), COOKING 15 MINS

450 g / 1 lb new potatoes, scrubbed
6 tbsp olive oil
3 tbsp white wine vinegar
1 dtsp lemon juice
sea salt flakes and ground black pepper
1 small clove of garlic, peeled and crushed

pinch brown sugar
a handful of mixed herbs such as rosemary, sage, parsley, thyme, tarragon, roughly chopped
50 g / 2 oz fresh grated Parmesan cheese, grated

Bring a large pan of water to the boil. Add the potatoes and simmer until they are done. A sharp knife should pass through them easily. Drain. While the potatoes are cooking make the dressing. Mix the olive oil, vinegar, lemon juice, salt and pepper, garlic, sugar and herbs together in a screw-top jar. Shake well. Pour over the warm potatoes. Mix well then sprinkle over the Parmesan. Leave for at least 5 minutes before eating.

DUCK BREAST WITH RADICCHIO AND CHINESE DRESSING

The combination of flavours and textures in this salad is just amazing. It's also delicious served with lashings of plum sauce.

SERVES 4, PREP 25 MINS, COOKING 20 MINS

1 duck breast
sea salt flakes and ground black pepper
2 tbsp olive oil
4 radicchio leaves
2 spring onions, chopped

a handful of green salad leaves
1 tbsp lemon juice
1 tsp soy sauce
1 cm / 1/2 in piece of fresh ginger, crushed

Preheat the oven to 200 °C / 400 °F / gas mark 6. Prick the duck breast all over with a skewer and pat dry with some kitchen paper. Sprinkle with a little salt. Heat the oil in a heavy-based preferably ovenproof pan. Cook the duck skin-side down over a medium-hot heat for approximately 2–4 minutes until golden brown and crispy. Transfer to an ovenproof dish and bake in the oven for 20 minutes. Tear the radicchio into pieces and toss in a bowl with the spring onions and salad leaves. Mix together the lemon juice, soy and ginger and season to taste. When the duck is cooked, leave it to relax cool for a few minutes, then slice thinly. Toss the pieces with the salad and pour the dressing over.

LENTIL AND SAUSAGE SALAD

Vegetarians can use goat's cheese in this recipe instead of sausages.

SERVES 4, PREP 15 MINS, COOKING 25 MINS

175 g / 6 oz puy lentils,
knob butter
1 small onion, finely chopped
1 stick celery, finely chopped
1 carrot, finely chopped
1 garlic clove, peeled and crushed
1 bay leaf
2 whole cloves
a sprig of thyme and rosemary
450 ml / 3/4 pint vegetable stock

FOR THE DRESSING
4 dtsp extra virgin olive oil
1 dtsp balsamic vinegar
1 tsp wholegrain mustard
squeeze of lemon juice
sea salt flakes and ground black pepper

6 good quality herb pork sausages,
cooked and sliced into chunks
Wholegrain or Dijon mustard to serve

Rinse the lentils and set aside. Melt the butter in a large pan and gently fry the onion, celery, carrot and garlic until they are translucent and are just turning brown. Add the lentils and stir well. Add the bay leaf, cloves, thyme and rosemary. Add the stock and bring to the boil. Cover the pan and simmer for 15–20 minutes.

Meanwhile, to make the dressing, mix together the olive oil, vinegar, mustard, lemon juice and salt and pepper. When the lentils are cooked they should have just a little liquid around them; if it seems excessive drain some off. Pour the dressing over and mix gently, seasoning to taste. Add the sausage chunks If serving immediately, otherwise, leave to cool then add the sausages. Serve with big dollops of mustard.

PRAWN SALAD WITH GARLIC AND CITRUS MAYONNAISE

This is a really delicious variation on prawn cocktail. If you're using frozen prawns let them defrost slowly in the fridge and drain them thoroughly. They should be plump and full of flavour. You can also buy ready-to-eat prawns from the fish section in most supermarkets.

SERVES 4, PREP 25 MINS

2 oranges
1 lemon
juice of 1 lime
1 small garlic clove, peeled and crushed
sea salt flakes and ground black pepper
2 tbsp flat leaf parsley, roughly chopped

3 tbsp good quality mayonnaise
125 ml / 4 fl oz double cream, lightly whipped or crème fraîche
175 g / 6 oz cooked peeled prawns
crisp green salad such as little gem and iceberg

Peel the oranges and lemon and remove the skin and white pith. Slice each fruit thinly, removing the pips as you go. Set aside. Mix together the lime juice, garlic, salt and pepper, parsley and mayonnaise, then gently stir in the cream or crème fraîche. Stir in the prawns. When you are ready to eat, mix in the citrus fruits and juice and serve with the salad leaves.

PRUNE, BACON AND SPINACH SALAD WITH BALSAMIC VINEGAR

Prunes and bacon are a classic combination. I often wrap bacon around prunes and dates and bake them until the bacon is crisp and the fillings soft in the middle. Pruneaux d'Agen are the best prunes you can buy, available from all good supermarkets – straight from France and ready to eat.

SERVES 4, PREP 15 MINS, COOKING 10 MINS

50 ml / 4¹/₂ tbsp olive oil
10 rashers smoky bacon, cut into little pieces
12 pruneaux d'Agen, roughly chopped

1 tbsp balsamic vinegar
225 g / 8 oz prepared baby spinach leaves
sea salt flakes and ground black pepper

Heat 30 ml / 2 tbsp of the oil in a wok or a large frying pan and sauté the bacon until crisp. Drain on kitchen paper. Add the prunes to the pan and sauté for 1 minute. Tip on to the paper with the bacon. Return the frying pan to the heat, add the remaining oil and the vinegar and scrape the base with a wooden spoon to dislodge any bits of bacon. Pour this sauce into a dish and leave to cool. To assemble the salad, toss the bacon and prunes through the spinach and drizzle over the sauce. Season to taste and pack into your lunchbox.

Alternatively, you could eat this salad hot if you are at home for lunch. Just pour the hot sauce on the spinach, add the bacon and prunes, season, mix well and voila!

ROQUEFORT, FRENCH BEAN AND HAZELNUT SALAD

Swap the green beans for sliced runner beans, waxy yellow beans or even broad beans for a change. You can even buy ready toasted chopped hazelnuts in most supermarkets. This is delicious with grilled meats, especially lamb, beef and chicken.

SERVES 4, PREP 15 MINS, COOKING 5 MINS

450 g / 1lb thin French beans
1 dtsp olive oil
1 dtsp lemon juice
175 g /6 oz Roquefort cheese, crumbled

50 g / 2 oz hazelnuts, toasted and roughly chopped
1 dtsp flat leaf parsley, roughly chopped
sea salt flakes and ground black pepper

Bring a large pan of water to the boil and cook the beans until they are just done – they should still have a little bite. Allow to cool slightly. Pour over the oil and lemon juice. Add the Roquefort to the beans with the hazelnuts. Sprinkle with parsley and season to taste.

SAFFRON RICE SALAD

Saffron is my favourite spice. I love the way that it magically transforms the colour and flavour of ingredients like rice.

SERVES 4, PREP 15 MINS, COOKING 10–15 MINS

350 g / 12 oz Basmati rice
pinch saffron threads
1 fennel bulb
4 ripe plum tomatoes

175 g / 6 oz frozen petit pois
juice of 1/2 lemon
1 tbsp olive oil
sea salt flakes and ground black pepper

Bring a large saucepan of water to the boil. Add the rice and the saffron, bring back to the boil and simmer for 10–15 minutes until it is cooked but still has a little bite. Drain and tip into a large bowl. While the rice is cooking, slice the fennel very thinly reserving the feathery fronds at the top. Cover the tomatoes with boiling water. Leave to stand for 1 minute, then drain and slip the skins off. Cut away the seeds and inner membranes and cut the flesh into slivers. Bring a small pan of water to the boil, add the petit pois and bring back to the boil. Drain and put in a bowl with the cooked saffron rice, lemon juice, olive oil, fennel and tomatoes and season to taste.

THAI PRAWN SALAD

This is really crisp and refreshing – perfect for summer. The fresh coriander and coconut milk make a wonderful dressing. If you want to make it more substantial serve it with cold Basmati or wild rice.

SERVES 4, PREP 15 MINS

175 g / 6 oz cooked peeled prawns
1 carrot
1 courgette
150 g / 5 oz beansprouts
1 red pepper
3 spring onions
1 fresh mild green chilli

FOR THE DRESSING
2.5 cm / 1 in piece of fresh root ginger, peeled and crushed
2 tbsp fresh coriander, roughly chopped
4 tbsp coconut milk
1 tbsp olive oil
1 tsp light soy sauce
juice of 1 lime
sea salt flakes and ground black pepper

Put the prawns in a large bowl. Peel the carrot and courgette and cut into very thin matchstick-sized julienne. Add to the bowl with the beansprouts. Seed the pepper, cut out the inner membranes and slice the flesh into thin strips. Remove the outer leaves from the spring onions and finely slice diagonally. Seed the chilli and chop finely. Add the pepper, onions and chilli to the prawns.

To make the dressing, mix together the ginger, coriander, coconut milk, olive oil, soy sauce and lime juice in a screw-top jar. Shake well. Pour over the salad, mix well and season to taste.

WHITE BEAN, TOMATO AND FRESH SAGE SALAD

Italian peasant food in a pot. It may seem a little bit basic for a recipe, but I still feel it should be included – who says we have to spend hours in the kitchen?

SERVES 4, PREP 20 MINS

2 x 400 g / 14 oz cans cannellini beans
4 ripe tomatoes, roughly chopped
a handful of fresh sage

FOR THE DRESSING
3 tbsp balsamic vinegar
juice of 1 lemon

2 tbsp extra virgin olive oil
1 tbsp Dijon mustard
2 shallots, peeled and finely chopped
sea salt flakes and ground black pepper

Put the beans, tomatoes and sage into a bowl. Mix all of the dressing ingredients together, drizzle over the beans and tomatoes. Season well and serve.

SALAD NIÇOISE

This is one of many people's all-time favourite salads. As with all of the salads using fresh tomatoes, this is best prepared in summer when tomatoes are ripe and at their peak.

SERVES 4, PREP 20 MINS, COOKING 15 MINS

125 g / 4 oz new potatoes
125 g / 4 oz French beans

FOR THE DRESSING
1 clove garlic, peeled and chopped
1 tbsp Dijon mustard
4 tbsp extra virgin olive oil
2 tbsp red wine vinegar

a handful of little gem lettuce leaves
200 g / 7 oz tuna fish
12 anchovies
5 vine ripened tomatoes, quartered
2 hard-boiled eggs, roughly chopped
a large handful of stoned black olives
fresh flat leaf parsley, roughly chopped
sea salt flakes and ground black pepper

Bring a pan of water to the boil and cook the potatoes until tender, add the beans just before the potatoes are cooked to blanch them. Drain the vegetables and thickly slice the potatoes. Transfer to a bowl.

To make the dressing, put all of the ingredients in a screw-top jar and shake well. Drizzle over the warm potatoes.

Tear the lettuce into bite-sized pieces and add to the bowl. Flake the tuna into large chunks and add to the bowl with the anchovies, tomatoes, eggs, olives and parsley. Carefully mix everything together. Season well and serve.

ONE-POT WONDERS

This section is all about complete meals in one pot that can easily be taken to work or enjoyed at home for lunch (or supper).

The key is to make more than one meal at one time. For example, make a dish of rice, add lots of vegetables and nuts and eat for supper; cool and chill any leftovers, add a jar of artichokes from the cupboard and you have lunch. Cook more pasta than you need at suppertime, chill overnight in a little olive oil; cook a few extra bacon rashers for breakfast, chop them and mix into the pasta with a small can of sweetcorn and some lumps of cheese, you have a lunch in 'one pot'. Similarly, when you are making your favourite dishes like kedgeree, make extra, leave to cool, pop some into a lunchbox and away you go. The good news is, to make these lunches in a pot, you're not spending any extra time in the kitchen.

If you are near a microwave at lunchtime, you could heat through many of these dishes and eat them hot, although, it has to be said that for the majority they are delicious cold.

Chose from blackened salmon with couscous, tarragon and lemon, chargrilled chicken with vegetables, or the recipe called 'everything from the fridge and more'! With the many new and exciting ingredients available to us, your lunchbox will never have looked or tasted so good. There's definitely a one-pot meal here for everyone.

PASTA TIPS

Dried pasta is fine for all the pasta recipes used in this section. It is often made from just flour and water – but not *any* flour. The best has a very high gluten content which allows it to cook *al dente* – firm to the bite. Look for a clear yellow colour and a label that tells you its made with semolina flour or durum wheat. A good pasta should not foam up when cooking.

Fresh pasta is not superior to dried pasta – they work differently with different sauces. Generally dried pasta works better with robust punchy sauces such as pepper and anchovy sauce, while fresh pasta suits more delicate sauces such as chicken and tarragon.

Choose the pasta shape to match the sauce. Tubes or shells work best with runnier sauces. Finer pastas like spaghetti or linguini are best with smoother sauces such as wild mushroom or tomato – you want the strands to stay separate and slippery. Ribbons and larger shapes are successful with chunkier sauces, chicken sauce for example.

To cook pasta, use the biggest pan you have – ideally you need about 4.5 litres / 8 pts of water for 450 g / 1 lb pasta. Bring to the boil, add the pasta, give it a quick stir, cover and bring back to the boil. Leave it uncovered at a good rolling boil until cooked. Drain.

Italians very rarely add any oil to the water. It's not necessary if you are going to mix the pasta and sauce immediately they are cooked. But if you are leaving the pasta sitting around, 15 ml / 1 tbsp oil added once it is cooked will help stop the pasta from sticking together.

Most importantly, do not overcook pasta. Remember, the only way to tell if it is cooked *al dente* is to taste it. Fresh pasta takes only about 1 minute to cook so watch it carefully. For dried pasta follow the packet instructions.

Aubergine, Mozzarella, tapenade and salami rolls

These are Mediterranean-style rolls that use thick slices of aubergine instead of bread. Ignore the aubergines' desperate cry for oil when you first start to cook them. After a couple of minutes they begin to release their own juices. This recipe will make twelve rolls, so the number of servings depends on how hungry you are.

SERVES 4–6, PREP 15 MINS, COOKING 10 MINS

2 large aubergines
2 tbsp extra virgin olive oil
125g / 4 oz tapenade
400 g / 14 oz Mozzarella, cut into 24 slices

24 slices of salami
a handful of fresh parsley, roughly chopped
sea salt flakes and ground black pepper

Cut the tops off the aubergines and cut each into 6 long strips. Brush with olive oil. Heat a griddle pan until really hot and griddle (or grill under a hot grill) for about 5 minutes on each side until golden and cooked. Place a piece of cooked aubergine on a board and spread with tapenade. Top with two slices of Mozzarella, two slices of salami and sprinkle with some fresh parsley. Roll the aubergine from the thin end. Put in a greaseproof sandwich bag and repeat with the other ingredients.

HERB AND LEMON PILAFF

I tend to use rice quite frequently in this book, probably because it is so delicious warm or cold. Remember to be really careful with cooked rice – keep the cold cooked rice in the fridge until you are ready for lunch and do not reheat. The flavours here are really subtle, the colours very pretty and the overall dish is a fabulous success. Cook it for supper and keep the rest for lunch. You could take a little extra fresh watercress in your lunchbox to munch alongside the rice.

SERVES 4, PREP 15 MINS, COOKING 20–25 MINS

2 tbsp olive oil
4 spring onions, sliced
2 green chillies, seeded and chopped
4 tbsp flat leaf parsley, roughly chopped
3 tbsp fresh coriander, roughly chopped
50 g / 2 oz fresh watercress

250 g / 9 oz long grain rice
juice and zest of 1 lemon
750 ml / 1 1/4 pt fresh chicken or vegetable stock
250 g / 9 oz fresh prawns, shelled but tails kept on
25 g / 1 oz butter
sea salt flakes and ground black pepper

Heat the oil in a large heavy-based saucepan, add the spring onions, chillies, half the herbs and half the watercress. Cook for 2 minutes, then add the rice and stir to combine. Add the lemon juice and zest. Add the stock and bring to the boil. Cover and simmer for 15 minutes. Add the prawns and cook for a further 3 minutes. Stir in the butter and fluff up the rice with a fork. Cook for 1 minute, then season to taste. Scatter the remaining herbs and watercress over the top.

CREAMY TARRAGON CHICKEN SERVED WITH BASMATI RICE OR NOODLES

I am not a fan of stock cubes so, if you cannot get hold of fresh chicken stock in your supermarket, use the equivalent amount of water and perhaps a splash of a good quality white wine. This sort of recipe is so versatile; you can serve the meal immediately or keep it chilled for a delicious lunch. If you have a microwave at work, keep the chicken and rice or noodles separate and heat only the chicken before serving.

SERVES 4, PREP 10 MINS, COOKING 15 MINS

25 g / 1 oz butter
4 chicken breasts, skinned, cut into thin strips
150 ml / 1/4 pt double cream
150 ml / 1/4 pt fresh chicken stock
198 g / 7 oz can sweetcorn
150 g / 5 oz sugar snap peas

15 g / 1/2 oz fresh tarragon
sea salt flakes and ground black pepper
juice of 1/2 lime
approx. 350 g / 12 oz cooked Basmati rice or noodles
1 lime, cut into wedges

Heat the butter in a large frying pan until melted. Add the chicken and sauté for about 5 minutes until the strips are golden on both sides. Add the cream and stock, bring to the boil and reduce the heat. Add the corn and sugar snap peas and half of the tarragon. Leave to cook gently for a few minutes. Season to taste. Add the lime juice to the rice or noodles with the remaining tarragon. Serve immediately or spoon the rice or noodles into a box, top with the creamy chicken and keep refrigerated until you are ready to eat. Serve with lime wedges.

THAI GREEN CURRY WITH CHICKEN AND VEGETABLES

You can make this intensely flavoured curry paste beforehand and store it in a screw-top jar for up to a week in the fridge. If time is short, use a bought Thai green curry paste. If you cannot find kaffir lime leaves, use lime zest instead. When I was researching this book, I asked many people to tell me their favourite lunchbox recipe; Thai green curry was a very popular choice. The great news about a recipe like this one is that the flavours develop over time so the dish actually improves if you can leave it overnight before eating.

SERVES 4, PREP 10 MINS, COOKING 15 MINS

FOR THE CURRY PASTE
5 medium/hot green chilli peppers, seeded and chopped
1 1/2 stems lemon grass, chopped
2 tbsp coriander leaves, chopped
1 tsp cumin seeds
2.5 cm / 1 in root ginger, peeled and chopped
4 springs onions, trimmed and roughly chopped
2 cloves garlic, peeled
1 tsp black peppercorns
1/2 tsp ground cinnamon
zest and juice of 1/2 lime

2 chicken breasts
2 tbsp groundnut oil
375 ml / 12 fl oz coconut milk
200 ml / 7 fl oz chicken stock
2 tbsp green curry paste (see above)
a pinch of salt
6 kaffir lime leaves
220 g / 9 oz fresh vegetables such as sugar snap peas, baby sweetcorn, peppers, peas
8 basil leaves, shredded

To make the curry paste, put all the ingredients in a food processor and whiz to a smooth purée. Cut the chicken into bite-sized pieces. Heat the oil and fry the chicken for about 2 minutes until golden. Bring the coconut milk and stock to the boil in a saucepan, stir in the curry paste and add the salt and lime leaves. Pour the warm coconut milk and stock over the chicken and simmer very gently for 10 minutes. Add the vegetables and cook for another couple of minutes until they are cooked but still have bite. Scatter the basil leaves over and serve or leave to cool.

LEMON CHICKEN ON RATATOUILLE

If you're cooking this for supper it can be served hot, but it's simply scrummy cold for lunch. Just spoon the cold ratatouille into a plastic container, scatter over some fresh basil leaves and top with the cold chicken strips. Seal and keep chilled until required. For vegetarians, simply marinate chunks of Feta cheese instead of chicken and spoon over the ratatouille.

SERVES 4, PREP 15 MINS (PLUS 2 HOURS MARINATING TIME), COOKING 25 MINS

4 chicken breasts
juice of 2 lemons
25 ml / 1 fl oz olive oil
sea salt flakes and ground black pepper

FOR THE RATATOUILLE
1 tbsp olive oil
1 onion, peeled and sliced
2 cloves garlic, peeled and crushed

1 aubergine, cut into chunks
1 red pepper, seeded and cut into chunks
450 g / 1 lb plum tomatoes, seeded and cut into chunks
2 small courgettes, cut into chunks
2 tbsp fresh basil leaves
sea salt flakes and ground black pepper

Put the chicken in a dish with the lemon juice and oil, season and leave to marinate for 2 hours. To make the ratatouille, heat the oil, add the onion and cook for 5 minutes. Add the garlic, aubergine and pepper chunks and cook for a further 8 minutes. Add the tomatoes and courgettes and cook for 8 minutes. Add the basil leaves and season well.

Heat a griddle or frying pan, add the chicken and its marinade and cook for 8–10 minutes on each side or until the chicken is cooked through. Slice the chicken diagonally and serve with the ratatouille.

MOROCCAN CHICKEN WITH PINE NUTS, SAFFRON AND SULTANAS

Some of my favourite ingredients are those used in Moroccan cooking – saffron, cinnamon, chilli and lemons to name but a few. Consequently, you will find that many of the recipes in this book include these ingredients in some shape or form. Like all of the recipes in *Lunchbox*, this one is versatile. If you don't fancy rice, make a bowl of the Moroccan chicken and take it to work with a big chunk of crusty bread. Whenever you see a chilling or marinating time just think of it as time to go and do something else: it doesn't mean that you need extra time in the kitchen!

SERVES 4, PREP 15 MINS (PLUS 1 HOUR CHILLING TIME), COOKING 15 MINS

1 red chilli pepper, seeded and diced
1 tsp crushed dried red chilli pepper
3 cloves garlic, peeled and finely chopped
juice of 1 lemon
2 tbsp olive oil
2 tsp ground cinnamon
pinch saffron or 2 tsp turmeric
125 g / 4 oz sultanas
75 g / 3 oz pine nuts, roughly chopped
450 g / 1 lb chicken pieces

FOR THE SAFFRON RICE
450 g / 1 lb Basmati rice
pinch saffron OR 5 ml/ 1 tsp turmeric)
fresh mint, to garnish

2 Spanish onions, peeled and sliced into strips
2 tbsp fresh mint, roughly chopped
2 tbsp fresh parsley, roughly chopped
sea salt flakes and ground black pepper

In a small bowl, mix together the fresh and dried chilli, garlic, lemon juice, half the olive oil, the cinnamon, saffron or turmeric, sultanas and pine nuts. Put the chicken in a shallow bowl and pour the chilli mixture over the top. Cover and refrigerate for at least 1 hour.

To make the saffron rice, bring a large pan of water to the boil, add the rice and saffron or turmeric and simmer uncovered for 12 minutes or until the rice is cooked. Drain.

Meanwhile, heat the remaining olive oil in a frying pan, add the chicken using a slotted spoon and the onion and cook over a high heat for about 5 minutes until golden. Turn over and cook the other side for a further 5 minutes or until the chicken is almost cooked. Add the marinade and bring to the boil. Simmer for 1 minute, then add the chopped herbs and season to taste. Either garnish with the mint leaves and serve immediately with the saffron rice or leave to cool, transfer to containers, scatter the mint over and keep refrigerated until you eat.

COUSCOUS WITH OLIVES AND FETA

There are so many ingredients that work well with couscous. As with pasta or any other staple carbohydrate, it relies on the ingredients you add to it for flavour and texture. In this case we are not serving the couscous with meat and vegetables, so we need a quick and simple method for cooking the grains. If you are cooking this for one, make up the whole recipe and keep any leftovers in the fridge. Add cooked sausages, chicken or tuna and you have another lunchbox or supper.

SERVES 4, PREP 15 MINS, COOKING 10 MINS

1 1/2 tbsp olive oil
25 g / 1 oz butter
2 large onions, peeled and sliced
1 tsp cumin seeds, toasted and
crushed
125 g / 4 oz sugar snap peas
1 tsp cayenne pepper

450 g / 1 lb couscous
75 g / 3 oz black olives
75 g / 3 oz green olives
125 g / 4 oz Feta cheese
juice of 1 lemon
2 tbsp mint, roughly chopped

Heat 15 ml / 1 tbsp of the oil and the butter in a large frying pan, add the onions and cumin and cook slowly for at least 20 minutes or until the onion has caramelised. Cook the peas in boiling water for 2 minutes, then drain. Put 600 ml / 1 pt water in a pan with the cayenne pepper and the remaining oil and heat gently. Add the couscous and stir with a wooden spoon. Remove from the heat, cover and leave for 5 minutes or until the water is absorbed. Add the onion mixture, return to the heat and cook gently for 3–4 minutes. Add the peas to the couscous mixture with the olives and cheese. Add the lemon juice and mint. Serve immediately or spoon into lunchboxes.

CHILLIED COUSCOUS WITH ROASTED VEGETABLES

Harissa paste is another storecupboard ingredient that everyone should have. It's based on hot red chilli peppers, olive oil and garlic, again often used in North African cooking. It's available in good supermarkets, but If you cannot get hold of any, add a seeded and chopped chilli pepper to the roasted vegetables instead.

SERVES 4, PREP 20 MINS, COOKING 45 MINS

450 g / 1 lb couscous
8 large vine ripened tomatoes
2 leeks, trimmed
3 courgettes
2 red peppers, seeded
1 yellow pepper, seeded
3 cloves of garlic

25 g / 1 oz butter
sea salt flakes and ground black pepper
2 tbsp harissa paste
a large handful of fresh coriander leaves, roughly chopped
a bunch of fresh basil leaves, roughly torn

Preheat the oven to 220 °C / 425 °F / gas mark 7. Put the couscous in a shallow ovenproof dish and pour over just enough warm water to cover the grains. Cover and put to one side. Pour boiling water over the tomatoes, leave for 20 seconds (any longer and the tomatoes will cook), then drain, plunge into a bowl of cold water and peel. Cut the tomato flesh into quarters. Diagonally slice the leeks and courgettes into thick chunks. Cut the peppers into big pieces. Put all the vegetables on a baking tray, drizzle over the oil, add the whole garlic cloves and bake for 45 minutes. Meanwhile, dot the butter over the couscous and season. Cover with foil and bake for 20 minutes alongside the vegetables. Fluff up the couscous with a fork, add the harissa paste, coriander leaves and roasted vegetables and mix together well. Scatter over the basil and spoon into lunchboxes.

CUMIN-SCENTED LAMB WITH APRICOTS
SERVED WITH COUSCOUS

In today's kitchen, ease and quickness of preparation are more important than they ever have been, which is why so many of these recipes are fast and simple. This is a fine example of a very basic recipe that provides a substantial lunch or supper. If you are cooking this dish for one, keep the lamb separate and freeze any left over, and the remaining couscous can beeaten as a side dish with an evening meal or add 25 g / 1 oz each of raisins and cashew nuts, a little honey and the juice of half of a lemon and you have another lunch in a pot!

SERVES 4, PREP 20 MINS, COOKING 25 MINS

1 tbsp olive oil
25 g / 1 oz butter
1 large onion, peeled and sliced
1 tsp cumin seeds, toasted and crushed
450 g / 1 lb lamb, cut into chunks

1 tsp cayenne pepper
1 tsp olive oil
250 g / 9 oz couscous
175 g / 6 oz ready-to-eat dried apricots

Heat the oil and butter in a large frying pan, add the onion and cumin and cook over a medium heat for 5 minutes. Add the lamb and cook for 20 minutes, turning frequently.

Meanwhile, put 225 ml / 9 fl oz water in a saucepan, add the cayenne pepper and oil and heat gently. Add the couscous and stir with a wooden spoon. Remove from the heat, cover and leave for 3 minutes or until the water is absorbed. Add the apricots and lamb mixture to the couscous. All you need is a tub to put it in, dust with a little cayenne pepper and it's ready to eat.

GARLIC LAMB SKEWERS WITH SAFFRON RICE

SERVES 4, PREP 15 MINS PLUS MARINATING TIME, COOKING 20 MINS

FOR THE KEBABS
700 g / 1 1/2 lb fillet end of leg of lamb or pieces
3 cloves garlic, peeled and finely chopped
1 tsp ground cinnamon
a pinch of saffron strands
5 tbsp olive oil
juice of 1 large lemon

sea salt flakes and ground black pepper
2 green peppers, seeded and cut into chunks

FOR THE SAFFRON RICE
450 g / 1 lb Basmati rice
a pinch of saffron strands

flat leaf parsley, to garnish

Cut the lamb into bite-sized pieces, place in a shallow bowl and add the garlic, cinnamon, saffron, oil and lemon juice. Mix well to coat all of the lamb and season well. Cover and leave to marinate for 6 hours or overnight. Thread the lamb and peppers alternately on to 8 skewers. Place under a preheated grill or on a hot barbecue for at least 20 minutes, turning occasionally and basting with the marinade, until the lamb is charred on the outside and slightly pink in the middle.

Meanwhile, to make the saffron rice, bring a large pan of water to the boil, add the rice and saffron and simmer uncovered for 12 minutes or until the rice is cooked. Drain. Serve the kebabs with the saffron rice and garnish with the flat leaf parsley.

SPINACH AND CREAMY GOAT'S CHEESE FRITTATA

Frittata is a delicious, thick, Italian omelette. The idea is to make the frittata for supper and keep a few pieces for tomorrow's lunch as it's delicious cut into wedges and served at room temperature with a little green salad. It's everything you need. Use milk instead of cream or a combination for a lighter frittata.

SERVES 4, PREP 10 MINS, COOKING 25 MINS

25 g / 1 oz butter
1 tbsp olive oil
1 red onion, peeled and sliced
150 g / 5 oz fresh baby spinach leaves
6 eggs

150 ml / 5 fl oz cream or milk
sea salt flakes and ground black pepper
150 g / 5 oz soft goat's cheese
a handful of fresh chives or parsley

Heat the butter and oil in a large frying pan, add the onion and sauté for 10–15 minutes or until golden brown, soft and caramelised. Add the spinach and cook for 1 minute.

Put the eggs and cream in a bowl, season well and whisk together. Pour the egg mixture over the onion and spinach mixture and cook for 8 minutes. It will still be runny in the centre. Dot the cheese over the top and put under a medium grill for 4 minutes or until golden and firm in the middle. Sprinkle with the herbs, cut into wedges and serve with a good chutney.

SLICES OF POTATO AND EGG

My brother's girlfriend is Spanish and every time she stays in England, she makes us something very similar to this for supper.

SERVES 4, PREP 10 MINS, COOKING 25 MINS

4 tbsp olive oil
4 onions, peeled and sliced
1.1 kg / 2½ lb large potatoes, peeled, halved lengthways and sliced
5 eggs, beaten

sea salt flakes and ground black pepper
a large handful of fresh herbs, roughly chopped
green salad, to serve

Heat the oil in a frying pan and add the onions and potato slices. Sauté for 5 minutes, stirring frequently. Cover and cook over a medium heat for a further 15 minutes or until tender, stirring occasionally. Preheat the grill. Season the eggs, add the herbs, then pour over the potato mixture in the frying pan. Cook over a low heat, shaking the pan until the omelette no longer sticks to the sides. Put under the grill for 5 minutes or until the top of the omelette is cooked and golden. Slice into wedges and serve warm with a fresh green salad.

EVERYTHING FROM THE FRIDGE AND MORE

This one is for my hairdresser, Brendan, who often takes a packed lunch to work. I asked him about the sort of food that he normally takes and he hit the nail on the head when he said that the best idea is to empty bits and pieces from your fridge into a large bowl and mix them with cold rice. Obviously, this can not be taken too literally – a pound of butter and a pint of milk may not be that appetising. However if you have a pot of salsa, chargrilled artichokes and tuna, this concept works very well. It was quite hard to write a recipe because anything goes. Just taste as you are adding different ingredients and add with sauces, relishes or spices as necessary.

SERVES 4, PREP 10 MINS

450 g / 1 lb Basmati rice, cooked
1 jar chargrilled artichokes
1 pot salsa
1 small can (approx. 113 g) sweetcorn, drained
1 small can tuna (approx. 113 g), drained

a handful of French beans or sugar snap peas
a handful of fresh herbs, roughly chopped
sea salt flakes and ground black pepper

Mix everything together in one pot, add a handful of fresh herbs if you have them and season to taste.

SPICY VEGETABLE CURRY

I really feel that it's essential to have some sort of curry in this section. We all know just how scrumptious curries can be, especially eaten with naan bread to soak up the sauce. It is advisable to make this the night before as the flavours blend together and improve with time. Coconut cream is pressed coconut that has a very thick and creamy texture. If you prefer, substitute coconut milk and omit the water from the recipe.

SERVES 10, PREP 20 MINS, COOKING 20 MINS

2 tbsp vegetable oil
2 large onions, peeled and sliced
7.5 cm / 3 in piece of fresh root ginger, peeled and finely chopped
3 cloves garlic, peeled and crushed
1 stick lemon grass, outer layer removed and finely sliced
1 green chilli, seeded and finely chopped

4 tsp medium curry powder
sea salt flakes and ground black pepper
900 g / 2 lb mixed green vegetables such as sugar snap peas and beans
300 ml / 10 fl oz coconut cream
300 ml / 10 fl oz water
a handful of fresh basil and coriander, roughly chopped

Heat the oil in a large saucepan. Add the onion, ginger, garlic and lemon grass and sauté gently for 10 minutes. Add the chilli and curry powder, season and cook for another 5 minutes. Add the vegetables, coconut cream and water to the saucepan and simmer gently for 15 minutes. Scatter the herbs over the top and serve.

SUSHI WITH PICKLED GINGER AND WASABI ON STICKY RICE

I adore sushi – I love the combination of fresh fish and sweet and sour rice. To prepare sushi at home you need to be sure that the fish you are using is completely fresh. This may sound obvious but it is critically important. Lots of people are still wary of eating fresh raw fish, so as a compromise I have marinated it in gin and lime juice first.

MAKES 15, PREP 15 MINS (PLUS 2 HOURS MARINATING TIME), COOKING 10 MINS

300 g / 11 oz salmon fillet
2 tbsp gin
juice of 1 lime
1 tbsp red peppercorns, crushed
450 ml / 3/4 pint water
a piece of dashi konbu seaweed

250 g / 8 oz Japanese rice for sushi
2 tbsp rice wine vinegar
2 tsp golden caster sugar
2 tsp approx. wasabi paste
3 tbsp pickled ginger

Remove any bones from the salmon. Place in a dish. Mix together the gin, lime juice and peppercorns and pour over the salmon. Leave for at least 2 hours. Slice the salmon into very thin strips using a sharp carving knife. Put the water, dashi konbu and rice in a large saucepan. Bring to the boil, remove the dashi konbu, cover and simmer for 10 minutes. Mix together the rice wine vinegar and sugar until the sugar has dissolved. Remove the rice from the heat, pour the vinegar and sugar mixture over and leave to stand, still covered, for 15 minutes. Transfer to a bowl and leave to cool. Mould the rice into little balls, top each with a little wasabi and pickled ginger, top with a slice of marinated salmon and serve.

SEARED SALMON WITH BEAN PURÉE AND PIMENTO DRESSING

If you want to make this one-pot even quicker, serve the salmon and potatoes with a creamy bought humus instead of the broad bean purée. The combination of soft and creamy purèe with fresh seared salmon and crunchy potatoes is just divine.

SERVES 4, PREP 20 MINS, COOKING 15 MINS

FOR THE BROAD BEAN PURÉE
125 g / 4 oz broad beans, cooked and shelled
juice of 2 lemons
2 fat cloves garlic, peeled and roughly chopped
4 tbsp olive oil
125 ml / 4 fl oz water
2 pimentos
50 ml / 2 fl oz Mascarpone cheese
sea salt flakes
cayenne pepper

2 salmon fillets

olive oil, for shallow-frying
sea salt flakes

FOR THE DRESSING
olive oil, for shallow-frying
4 new potatoes, cubed
2 pimentos, roughly chopped
juice of 1 lemon
2 tbsp olive oil
2 tbsp fresh flat leaf parsley, roughly chopped
sea salt flakes and ground black pepper

8 cos lettuce leaves

To make the broad bean purée, put the beans, lemon juice, garlic, olive oil, water and pimentos in a food processor and blend until smooth. Stir in the

197

Mascarpone and season with salt and cayenne pepper.

Heat a frying pan, add a little olive oil and sear the salmon for 2 minutes on each side or until almost cooked through. Season with salt and transfer to a plate.

To make the dressing, add a little more olive oil to the salmon pan, add the potato cubes and sauté for 3–4 minutes or until crispy and golden. Remove from the pan and reserve. Add the chopped pimentos and lemon juice to the frying pan and stir to deglaze. Add the olive oil and parsley and cook for 1 minute. Remove from the heat and season to taste.

Arrange 2 lettuce leaves each on four plates or in four lunchboxes, followed by a spoonful of the broad bean purée. Slice both salmon fillets and arrange a few slices on top of the salad. Scatter the potatoes over, drizzle over the dressing from the pan and serve.

BAKED CITRUS SALMON WITH COUSCOUS AND TOMATOES

At the risk of beginning to sound like a stuck record, I emphasise yet again that all of these recipes are versatile. If you don't have fresh salmon, use another fish instead. Likewise, if you do not eat fish, make the recipe without it but add a handful of fresh vegetables of your choice instead.

SERVES 4, PREP 10 MINS, COOKING 15–20 MINS (DEPENDING ON THE THICKNESS OF THE SALMON)

450 g / 1 lb couscous
4 tomatoes, roughly chopped
a bunch of mint, roughly chopped
a bunch of dill, roughly chopped
1 clove of garlic, peeled and roughly chopped

zest and juice of 1 orange
sea salt flakes and ground black pepper
3 tbsp olive oil
3 tbsp white wine or water
4 salmon fillets, skinned
a bunch of fresh basil leaves

Preheat the oven to 220 °C / 425 °F / gas mark 7. Put the couscous in a shallow ovenproof dish and just cover with warm water. Leave for 5 minutes. Throw the tomatoes, half the mint and dill, the garlic, orange zest, oil and wine or water in a bowl, mix together, and season. Add the remaining mint and dill to the couscous with the orange juice. Arrange the salmon on top of the couscous, spoon the tomato mixture over and cover with foil. Bake for 15 minutes until the couscous is warm and the salmon cooked through. Scatter over the basil leaves, spoon on to warmed serving plates and serve, or leave to cool and take for lunch.

CHARGRIDDLED CHICKEN WITH SALSA VERDE

Salsa verde is a vivid green, fabulously pungent sauce, traditionally served with *bollito mista* – a northern Italian dish of boiled meats and poultry. This quantity of sauce is more than you need, keep any left over in a screw-top jar in the fridge and use with meat or tossed over freshly cooked potatoes within a few days.

SERVES 4, PREP 15 MINS, COOKING 10 MINS

FOR THE SALSA VERDE
75 g / 3 oz flat leaf parsley, stalks removed
125 g / 4 oz fresh mint
125 g / 4 oz fresh basil
2 cloves of garlic
1 tbsp Dijon mustard
5 anchovy fillets

2 tbsp capers
125 ml / 4 fl oz extra virgin olive oil
juice and rind of 1 lemon

4 chicken breasts
2 tbsp olive oil
4 courgettes, diagonally sliced

To make the salsa verde, put all the ingredients except the oil and lemon juice in a food processor and whiz until smooth. Gradually add the oil and lemon juice.

Put the chicken breasts in a plastic bag and bash with a rolling pin to flatten. Brush a griddle pan with the oil and heat until really hot. Cook the chicken for about 5 minutes on each side until cooked through and golden on the outside. Transfer to a plate and slice. Add the courgettes to the griddle pan and griddle for 5 minutes on each side. Spoon the courgettes on to plates or into pots, cover with the sliced chicken and spoon the salsa verde over the top.

ROASTED VINE RIPENED TOMATOES WITH FRESH LIME AND SALSA VERDE

Roasting the tomatoes intensifies their sweet, tomato flavour, which provides an amazing contrast to the fresh salsa verde and lime juice. A pot of this for lunch is perfect. You can always toss some freshly cooked rice into the tomato and sauce mixture to make it slightly more filling.

SERVES 4, PREP 15 MINS, COOKING 25 MINS

450 g / 1 lb vine ripened tomatoes, roughly chopped
2 cloves of garlic
juice of 1 lime

sea salt flakes and ground black pepper
extra virgin olive oil
1 quantity salsa verde (see page 200)
wild rocket leaves, to serve

Preheat the oven to 200 °C / 400 °F / gas mark 6. Place the tomatoes in an ovenproof dish with the garlic. Sprinkle the lime juice over, season and drizzle with olive oil. Roast for 20 minutes. Spoon the tomatoes into a serving bowl or container and either drizzle the salsa verde over the top or carry separately. Scatter some fresh wild rocket leaves over the top and eat at room temperature or heat in a microwave before serving.

JAPANESE TUNA WITH NOODLES AND WASABI

Wasabi is a Japanese horseradish with attitude and it is a fine example of an unusual ingredient that is now readily available in supermarkets. You can normally buy it as a paste in a tube or as a powder to which you add water. The longer you can leave the marinade the better – you can throw everything together in the evening and cook the tuna quickly before you go to work or when you pop home for lunch.

SERVES 4, PREP 15 MINS (PLUS 6 HOURS MARINATING TIME), COOKING 2–3 MINS

100 ml / 3½ fl oz light soy sauce, plus extra to taste
50 ml / 2 fl oz saké
1 tbsp freshly grated root ginger
2 tsp unrefined golden brown sugar

700 g / 1½ lb fresh tuna, cut into 2.5 cm / 1 in cubes
300 g / 11 oz rice noodles
2 tbsp pickled ginger
2 tsp wasabi paste

Put the soy sauce, saké, ginger and sugar in a bowl. Add the tuna and leave to marinate for at least 6 hours. Drain away the marinade and discard. Heat a griddle pan or heavy-based frying pan and flash-fry the tuna for 45 seconds on each side (it will still be rare in the middle). Put to one side. Soak or cook the rice noodles according to the packet instructions. When cool, toss, add a little soy sauce to taste and the pickled ginger. Toss again. Divide the noodles between containers and top with the tuna. Take the wasabi with you and serve a little with each portion.

SALT-CRUSTED SALMON WITH A MANGO SALSA

This recipe can be cooked outside if you are fortunate enough to have an outdoor lunch break. If you cook the salmon on a barbecue it will be crisp and smoky on the outside and succulent in the middle. The salsa is soft and fruity.

SERVES 4, PREP 20 MINS, COOKING 10–15 MINS

FOR THE SALSA
1 mango, peeled and stoned
1 red onion, peeled and diced
6 vine ripened tomatoes, seeded and diced
$1/2$ green chilli, seeded and diced
1 tbsp coriander, roughly chopped
2 tbsp white wine vinegar

FOR THE SALMON
4 salmon steaks approx. 120 g / $4^1/2$ oz
1 tbsp sea salt flakes
freshly ground black pepper
2 tbsp olive oil

1 lime, cut into wedges, to serve

To make the salsa, dice the mango flesh and put in a small bowl. Add the remaining ingredients, mix together well and refrigerate for 20 minutes.

Place the salmon steaks in a dish, sprinkle over the salt and season with freshly ground black pepper. Heat the oil in a heavy-based frying pan and sear the salmon on one side for 3 minutes. Turn over and continue to cook for at least 10 minutes or until the salmon is cooked. Spoon the salsa into pots, top with the salmon and serve with lime wedges to squeeze over.

BLACKENED SALMON WITH COUSCOUS

Use a different fish if you prefer. The combination of spices here may seem scary but the flavours are not too strong once they are crushed and cooked until crisp.

SERVES 4, PREP 10 MINS, COOKING 5 MINS

225 g / 8 oz couscous
extra virgin olive oil, for drizzling
juice of 1 lime
a handful of fresh coriander leaves,
roughly chopped
1 tsp cayenne pepper
1 tsp ground coriander
1 tsp garam masala (see page 16 or
use bought)

1 tsp cumin seeds
1 tsp ground black pepper
1 tsp fennel seeds
1 tsp sea salt
4 x 125 g / 4 oz salmon fillets
sunflower oil, for shallow frying

Pour warm water over the couscous to just cover the grains. Cover and leave for 10 minutes. Season, drizzle over oil and the lime juice and fluff up with a fork. Add the coriander and mix well. Grind together all the spices and the salt with a pestle and mortar. Coat the salmon in the spices. Heat the sunflower oil in a frying pan until hot and smoking. Cook the fillets on each side until blackened. Serve the salmon on a bed of the couscous with a few coriander leaves on top.

COURGETTES WITH LEMON AND ROSEMARY

This looks so pretty – a big pile of fresh green strips of courgette mixed through pasta and served with bright chunks of lemon and rosemary. The delicate flavours of the rosemary and lemon enhance the courgette beautifully.

SERVES 4, PREP 20 MINS, COOKING 15 MINS

450 g / 1 lb spaghetti
700 g / 1 1/2 lb courgettes
2 tbsp olive oil
1 garlic clove, peeled
2 sprigs rosemary

Grated rind of 1/2 lemon
sea salt flakes and ground black pepper
5 tbsp double cream
rosemary leaves and lemon wedges, to
serve

Cook the pasta in a large pan of boiling water and drain. Cut the courgettes into very thin rounds by hand or with the large cutters on a grater (they look pretty if they are cut at a slight angle). Heat the oil in a large frying pan. Crush the garlic slightly by bashing with a rolling pin or the back of a large knife and add to the oil with the rosemary. Sauté gently for a couple of minutes, without allowing it to brown. Remove the garlic, add the courgettes and lemon rind and cook for a few minutes. Remove the rosemary, season well and stir in the cream. Serve the sauce over the freshly cooked pasta with a lemon wedge and a little fresh rosemary on top. Alternatively, leave the sauce to cool, spoon the pasta into lunchboxes, pour the sauce over and take to work.

A RICH MUSHROOM SAUCE FOR PASTA

This is a quick pasta dish as long as you remember to soak the porcini mushrooms for 30 minutes beforehand. You should allow 75–125 g / 3–4 oz dried or fresh pasta per person for a main course. I adore this sauce, there are so many ways of serving it. Try it with bread, on new or mashed potatoes, or on a creamy pile of polenta. if you are feeding a family, add a few more mushrooms to the dish, serve some for supper and keep the rest for lunch the next day.

SERVES 4, PREP 20 MINS (PLUS 30 MINS SOAKING TIME), COOKING 30 MINS

15 g / ½ oz dried porcini mushrooms
550 g / 1¼ lb open-cap mushrooms
50 g / 2 oz butter
½ medium onion, peeled and finely chopped
1 clove garlic, peeled and crushed

1 tbsp Marsala or brandy (optional)
450 g / 1 lb tagliatelle
a handful of fresh flat leaf parsley, roughly chopped
sea salt flakes and ground black pepper

Cover the porcini mushrooms with 300 ml / 10 fl oz boiling water and leave to soak for 30 minutes. Chop the open-cap mushrooms into little pieces. Heat the butter in a frying pan, add the onion and sauté for a few minutes until golden. Add the garlic and sauté for 1 minute. Drain the porcini mushrooms, reserving the liquor, and chop finely. Add to the onion with the open-cap mushrooms. Cook slowly for 20 minutes. Add the reserved mushroom stock, the Marsala or brandy, if using, and reduce for a few minutes. Meanwhile, bring a large pan of water to the boil, add the pasta and cook. Drain. Add the pasta to the sauce with the parsley. Season to taste, toss everything together and serve.

TOMATO AND MOZZARELLA PASTA

Adding the pasta while it is still hot to the cheese and tomato mixture has the wonderful effect of melting the cheese so that the end result is gooey and divine. Keep it simple – it always works.

SERVES 4, PREP 15 MINS (PLUS 20 MINS MARINATING), COOKING 10–12 MINS (FOR THE PASTA)

300 g / 11 oz vine ripened tomatoes
250 g / 9 oz Mozzarella cheese,
roughly chopped
4 tbsp extra virgin olive oil
1 tbsp shredded fresh basil

450 g / 1 lb conchiglie rigate
(pasta shells)
sea salt flakes and ground black pepper
a handful of fresh basil leaves

Pour boiling water over the tomatoes, leave for 20 seconds, then drain. Peel the tomatoes, remove the seeds and roughly chop the flesh. Place in a bowl with the cheese and drizzle the oil over. Scatter the shredded basil over and leave to marinate for 20 minutes. Meanwhile, bring a large pan of water to the boil and cook the pasta. Drain. While the pasta is still hot, add it to the cheese and tomato, mix together well and season. Scatter the basil leaves over the top and serve or pack for lunch.

SAUTÉED PEPPERS, ANCHOVIES AND LOTS OF HERBS

This sauce will not need seasoning with salt as the anchovy fillets are salty. Remember, there are always ways to reduce the amount of time spent in the kitchen: if you do not have time to roast the peppers yourself, pick up a pot of roasted peppers from the supermarket or deli. Serve this dish warm for lunch or supper or leave out the pasta, allow the pepper mixture to go cold and spread thickly on to bread and serve with a fresh green salad.

SERVES 4, PREP 20 MINS, COOKING 20 MINS

3 red peppers
2 yellow peppers
450 g / 1 lb pasta
2 tbsp olive oil
2 cloves of garlic, peeled and crushed
1/2-1 tsp crushed red chilli peppers
50 g / 2 oz anchovy fillets in oil, drained and chopped

6 tbsp Cirio Rustica roughly chopped tomatoes
2 tbsp flat leaf parsley, roughly chopped
ground black pepper

Preheat grill to high, cut the peppers in half, put on a baking tray skin side up and grill until the skins turn black (this takes about 10 minutes). Put the peppers in a plastic bag (the steam helps to loosen the skin) peel and slice into thin strips. While the peppers are grilling, cook the pasta in lots of boiling water and drain. Heat the oil, add the garlic and chilli and sauté for 3–4 minutes. Add the anchovies, peppers and tomatoes and cook for a few more minutes. Add the pasta, parsley, and season with pepper. Toss everything together and serve.

KING PRAWNS, STRAW MUSHROOMS AND NOODLES

With ingredients like straw mushrooms and water chestnuts available in cans, you can make dishes like this one so easily.

SERVES 4, PREP 10 MINS, COOKING 10 MINS

250 g / 8 oz pack of medium egg noodles
15ml / 1 tbsp olive oil
1 clove garlic, peeled and crushed
5 cm / 2 in piece of root ginger, peeled and grated
350 g / 12 oz king prawns, shelled but tails kept on

2 tbsp soy sauce
125 g / 4 oz can bamboo shoots
125 g / 4 oz water chestnuts, sliced
225 g / 8 oz broccoli, cut into florets
400 g / 14 oz can straw mushrooms (or champignons)
2 spring onions, finely sliced, to garnish

Cook the noodles according to the packet instructions. Drain and put to one side. Heat the oil in a wok or large saucepan, add the garlic and ginger and cook for 1 minute. Add the prawns and cook for about 3 minutes until tender and pale pink in colour. Add the soy sauce, bamboo shoots, water chestnuts, broccoli and straw mushrooms, toss everything together and cook for 1 minute. Garnish with the spring onions and serve.

CANTONESE NOODLES

Make up the peanut satay recipe or use bought. I love the combination of peanuts, chicken and noodles and this whole dish keeps really well – in fact it improves overnight, giving the flavours time to develop.

SERVES 4, PREP 10 MINS (PLUS 30 MINS MARINATING), COOKING 5 MINS

450 g / 1 lb boneless chicken breast, cut into thin strips
1 quantity of peanut satay sauce (see page 72)
125 g / 4 oz baby corn, halved lengthways and trimmed to 5 cm / 2 inches

125 g / 4 oz asparagus spears, halved lengthways and cut into 5 cm / 2 inch strips
175 g / 6 oz thin noodles
50 g / 2 oz peanuts or cashew nuts
2 tsp peanut oil
a handful of fresh coriander leaves

Marinade the chicken in the peanut satay sauce for 30 minutes. Remove from the marinade and thread on to bamboo skewers. Cook under a grill or on a griddle for 5 minutes until the chicken is tender and cooked through, turning halfway through cooking.

Meanwhile, bring a large pan of salted water to the boil, add the baby sweet-corn, asparagus and thin noodles and cook for 3 minutes. Drain. Add the nuts, oil, coriander and chicken and toss everything together. Serve, or spoon the noodles into pots and top with the chicken strips. Serve with any remaining satay sauce.

ROASTED TOMATO, CHÈVRE AND TAPENADE TARTS

Chèvre or goat's cheese is soft and creamy with a delicious flavour. Alternatively, use a soft cream cheese. I have made very quick tapenade here, but to save time you could buy a pot or use a pesto or tomato purée instead.

SERVES 4, PREP 20 MINS, COOKING 45 MINS

375 g / 13 oz puff pastry
125 g / 4 oz yellow tomatoes
125 g / 4 oz cherry tomatoes
125 g / 4 oz plum tomatoes
2 tbsp olive oil
sea salt flakes and ground black pepper

FOR THE TAPENADE
2 tbsp capers, rinsed
2 cloves garlic, peeled and chopped
4 anchovy fillets, rinsed
225 g / 8 oz black olives, stoned
2 tsp olive oil
175 g / 6 oz Chèvre
black olives and basil leaves, to garnish

Preheat the oven to 200 °C / 400 °F / gas mark 6. Roll out the pastry to about 6 mm / 1/4 in thick. Cut four 10 cm / 4 in squares and use the leftover pastry to form borders by cutting into 10 mm / 1/3 in strips and placing them around the edges of the pastry. Place on greased baking sheets. Put all the tomatoes in a roasting tin. Drizzle with the olive oil, season with salt and pepper and cook for 45 minutes. To make the tapenade, pound the capers, garlic and anchovy fillets together with a pestle and mortar until crushed. Add the olives a few at a time, crushing thoroughly but stopping before the mixture becomes slushy. Add the olive oil and spoon into the pastry squares. Cover the olive tapenade with cubes of goat's cheese and top with the roasted tomatoes. Cook the tarts in the oven for 20 minutes until the pastry is puffy and golden brown. Scatter over black olives and fresh basil leaves.

TARRAGON AND LEMON CHARGRIDDLED CHICKEN WITH VEGETABLES

Bashing the chicken with a rolling pin tenderises the meat and makes it much quicker to cook. If you have not already invested in a griddle pan, you must buy one, but it need not be very expensive.

SERVES 4, PREP 20 MINS, COOKING 15 MINS

4 chicken breasts
a handful of fresh tarragon
4 tbsp olive oil
sea salt flakes and ground black pepper
2 lemon wedges

1 red pepper, grilled
1 courgette, thinly sliced diagonally
1 fennel bulb, sliced
1 red onion, cut into wedges
6 cherry tomatoes, halved

Bash the chicken with a rolling pin to flatten and put it in a shallow dish. Scatter over the tarragon and half the olive oil and season. Cover and put to one side. Peel the grilled pepper and cut the flesh into strips. Heat a heavy-based griddle pan or frying pan on a high heat and cook the chicken breasts for a couple of minutes on each side. Squeeze the lemon wedges over. Place in between two warmed plates and put to one side. Arrange the vegetables in the same pan and drizzle with the remaining oil. Cook in the oven for 10 minutes, turning frequently. Spoon the vegetables into pots or on to plates and top with the chicken, sliced if wished.

SCALLOP KEBABS WITH CHARGRILLED COCONUT AND MANGO SALSA

This has to be eaten to be believed. It's a taste of lots of different countries all in one mouthful. The juicy scallops and prawns marinated in a cardamom and coconut sauce is delicious with the soft fresh fruits and mint.

SERVES 4, PREP 20 MINS (PLUS 30 MINS, MARINATING TIME), COOKING 5 MINS

FOR THE MANGO SALSA
2 tbsp orange juice
2 tbsp soft brown sugar
1 tsp ground cinnamon
seeds from 3 cardamom pods
4 mangoes peeled, stoned and sliced
2 pawpaw peeled, seeded and sliced
75 g / 3 oz coconut flakes, toasted
1 tbsp fresh mint leaves

FOR THE KEBABS
400 ml can coconut milk
1 red chilli, seeded and sliced
5 lime leaves
sea salt flakes and ground black pepper
16 tiger prawns
16 scallops

1/2 cucumber, sliced into long thin ribbons
zest of 1 lime

To make the salsa, mix together the orange juice, brown sugar, cinnamon and crushed cardamom seeds in a bowl. Add the mango and pawpaw slices and coat well with the orange juice mixture. Cover and leave to marinate for 30 minutes. To prepare the fish kebabs, pour the coconut milk into a large shallow dish and add the chilli, lime leaves and seasoning. Thread the prawns and scallops on to wooden skewers and place in the coconut marinade. Cover and chill for 30 minutes.

213

Griddle or grill the fish for 2 minutes on each side or until the prawns and scallops are cooked through. Add the toasted coconut flakes and mint leaves to the salsa. To serve, arrange a little pile of cucumber ribbons on four plates, top each with the kebabs, spoon the salsa by the side and scatter over the lime zest.

Pour the coconut milk into a large shallow dish, add the chilli, lime leaves and seasoning. Thread the prawns and scallops on to wooden skewers. Put the kebabs into the coconut marinade, cover and chill for 30 minutes. Griddle or grill the fish for 2 minutes each side or until cooked through. Add the toasted coconut flakes to the salsa, serve with the kebabs.

FETA AND SPINACH PIE

Filo pastry is very easy and quick to use and the end results look so effective. If you have any filo left over, it can safely be refrozen because there is no fat in it. Serve this pie with a fresh tomato salad or sauce for the perfect lunch.

SERVES 4, PREP 25 MINS, COOKING 30 MINS

2 tbsp olive oil
I small white onion, peeled and finely chopped
I clove garlic, peeled and crushed
250 g / 9 oz frozen spinach, thawed
125 g / 4 oz red lentils, cooked
75 g / 3 oz Feta cheese, crumbled

75 g / 3 oz Cheddar cheese, grated
I tbsp freshly chopped mint
1/4 tsp ground nutmeg
freshly ground black pepper
I tbsp olive oil
chives, to garnish

Heat 15 ml / 1 tbsp of the oil in a non-stick frying pan over a medium heat. Fry the onion and garlic gently for 5 minutes, stirring frequently. Add the spinach and cook for a further 3 minutes, stirring continuously. Spoon the spinach mixture into a bowl, add the lentils, Feta, Cheddar, mint, nutmeg and pepper to taste. Preheat the oven to 180 °C / 350 °F / gas mark 5. Lightly grease a 23 cm / 9 in pie dish with a little of the remaining oil. Layer three sheets of filo pastry, brushing each with oil. Place the pastry across the pie dish and repeat with the remaining six sheets of pastry. Spoon the cheese mixture into the dish and fold the overhanging strips of pastry over the filling. Scrunch the ends together and brush with oil. Bake in the preheated oven for 30 minutes until crisp and golden. Garnish with chives and serve in chunks.

Satay lamb kebabs

If the weather is good enough, cook these on the barbecue until charred and cooked through. Pitta bread is a great lunchbox friend: cut a slit down one side to make a pocket and you can put almost anything inside.

Serves 4, Prep 20 mins (plus 1 hour marinating time), Cooking 1 hour

FOR THE MARINADE
2 tbsp soy sauce
2 tbsp peanut butter
90 ml / 3 fl oz coconut milk
1 garlic clove, peeled and crushed
1 red chilli, seeded and finely chopped
OR 1/4 tsp dried red chilli flakes
2 tsp soft brown sugar

700 g / 1 1/2 lb lamb neck fillets
12 plump spring onions, cut into bite-size pieces
1 green or yellow pepper, seeded and cut into 2 cm / 3/4 inch pieces
24 red cherry tomatoes
4 pitta breads (optional)

To make the marinade, put the soy sauce, peanut butter, coconut milk, garlic, chilli and sugar in a small bowl and mix together well. Trim the lamb and cut into 2 cm / 3/4 in pieces. Arrange in a single layer in a shallow ovenproof dish. Pour the marinade over and stir to coat evenly. Cover and chill in the refrigerator for at least 1 hour.

Soak 12 long bamboo skewers in cold water for at least 10 minutes. Preheat the grill to high. Thread the lamb, spring onions and pepper pieces on the skewers, dividing them equally. Place a cherry tomato on the end of each of the skewers. Cook for 15–20 minutes, turning once or twice, until the meat is tender and golden brown.

EASY AUBERGINE BAKE

This is a perfect recipe for vegetarians, but it also makes an excellent accompaniment to grilled lamb chops or roasted chicken. To cut the aubergines for this recipe, cut a strip lengthways off the bottom, so that the aubergine lies flat on a surface, then slice into long, thin strips.

SERVES 4, PREP 35 MINS, COOKING 35 MINS

3 tbsp olive oil
4 aubergines, cut lengthwise into 1 cm / 1/2 in slices
400 g / 14 oz can butter beans, drained
juice of 1 lemon
1 clove garlic, peeled and crushed
1 onion, peeled and finely chopped

400 g / 14 oz can chopped tomatoes
3 tbsp tomato purée
a handful of basil leaves, roughly torn
sea salt flakes and ground black pepper
125 g / 4 oz breadcrumbs
a handful of fresh parsley and basil, roughly torn

Preheat the oven to 230 °C / 450 °F / gas mark 8. Brush two baking sheets with a little of the olive oil. Place the long aubergine slices on the baking sheets and brush with oil. Season and bake for 10–15 minutes until almost cooked through but not browned. Mash the beans and lemon juice to a purée. Heat a little of the oil and fry the garlic and onion gently for 5 minutes, then add the mashed beans and mix together. Put the chopped tomatoes into a small saucepan and stir in the tomato purée.

Cook over a low heat, stirring often, until the sauce has thickened slightly, then add the basil and seasoning. Spoon some of the tomato sauce into an ovenproof dish, cover with a layer of aubergine slices and top these with the butter bean purée. Repeat with the remaining aubergine slices and butter bean mixture.

Finish with a layer of tomato sauce and sprinkle with the fresh breadcrumbs. Reduce the oven temperature to 200 °C / 400 °F / gas mark 6 and bake for 20 minutes or until completely heated through and the breadcrumbs are browned and crispy. Scatter over the fresh herbs and serve.

SPINACH PESTO BEANS

Serve these beans on toast for a quick lunch or on jacket potatoes to make them into a supper. If you have other herbs or nuts that need using, use them to make the pesto instead of the basil and pine nuts. If you want to make double the quantity of pesto, it keeps in the fridge for a few days in a screw-top jar.

SERVES 4, PREP 10 MINS, COOKING 5 MINS

3 cloves garlic, peeled and roughly chopped
50 g / 2 oz fresh spinach leaves
40 g / 1 1/2 oz basil leaves
sea salt flakes and ground black pepper
50 g / 2 oz pine kernels

25 g / 1 oz Parmesan cheese, grated
6 tbsp extra virgin olive oil
2 x 400 g cans cannellini beans
basil leaves and Parmesan shavings, to garnish

Put the garlic, spinach and half of the basil leaves in a food processor, add a pinch of salt and whiz to a paste. Add the pine nuts and Parmesan and purée until smooth. With the machine still running, gradually add the oil until a smooth paste is formed. Put the pesto into a saucepan, add the beans and heat gently until warmed through. Serve warm with the extra basil leaves and Parmesan shavings on top.

EAT AT HOME PIZZAS

I have specified to eat at home simply because when I asked friends if they would eat pizzas cold, the general response was negative. However, I disagree. A cold slice of tomato, Mozzarella and basil pizza smothered in mayonnaise can be incredibly tasty and filling. They each serve 3 or 4, depending on how hungry you are.

TOMATO, MOZZARELLA AND BASIL

Keep it simple – the only other ingredient that we could add to this pizza is a bundle of fresh rocket leaves.

SERVES 4, PREP 10 MINS, COOKING 15 MINS

20 cm / 8 in pizza base
4 tbsp tomato passata
5 plum tomatoes, thinly sliced

200 g / 7 oz Mozzarella cheese, thinly sliced
a handful of fresh basil, roughly torn

Preheat the oven to 220 °C / 425 °F / gas mark 7. Put the base on a baking tray, spread with the passata, arrange the tomato slices on top, followed by the cheese. Cook for 15 minutes or until the base is golden and the cheese melted. Scatter the basil leaves over, slice and serve.

LAMB WITH ONIONS AND PEPPERONI

This is just delicious. Cayenne pepper is ground from small red chilli peppers of the *Capsicum frutescens* variety, whereas ground chilli powder may contain other spices such as cumin, oregano and allspice as well. It is perfect for adding heat to dishes from curries and Mexican dishes to cheese and egg dishes; without the normal inconvenience of chopping and preparing fresh chillies. It is a good idea to keep a little pot of cayenne on the kitchen table and use it to add a little extra flavour to dishes once cooked.

SERVES 4, PREP 15 MINS, COOKING 40 MINS

1 tbsp vegetable oil
2 Spanish onions, peeled and sliced
450 g / 1 lb minced lamb

1 tsp cayenne pepper
5 tbsp tomato passatta
125 g / 4 oz pepperoni, sliced

Preheat the oven to 220 °C / 425 °F / gas mark 7. Heat the oil in a frying pan, add the onions and sauté for 10 minutes or until golden and cooked. Add the lamb and sauté for about 10 minutes until browned and the grains are separated. Add the cayenne pepper and passata, mix together and continue to cook for a few more minutes. Spoon the lamb mixture on to the pizza base on a baking tray, add the peperoni slices and cook for 15 minutes.

EGG, SPINACH AND PARMESAN CHEESE PIZZA

SERVES 4, PREP 10 MINS, COOKING 15 MINS

20 cm / 8 in pizza base
200 g / 7 oz spinach

1 egg
40 g / 1 1/2 oz fresh Parmesan cheese

Preheat the oven to 220 °C / 425 °F / gas mark 7. Heat a large wok or frying pan, add the spinach and cook for a couple of minutes until wilted. Roughly chop and scatter over the pizza base on a baking tray. Crack the egg into the middle and scatter the Parmesan over the top. Bake for 15 minutes or until the egg and the pizza base are both cooked.

PRAWN AND FETA CHEESE PIZZA

SERVES 4, PREP 15 MINS, COOKING 15 MINS

1 tbsp oil
2 red onions, peeled and cut into wedges
20 cm / 8 in pizza base

125 g / 4 oz Feta cheese, crumbled
sea salt flakes and ground black pepper
125 g / 4 oz large cooked prawns

Preheat the oven to 220 °C / 425 °F / gas mark 7. Heat the oil in a large frying pan, add the onions and sauté for 5 minutes. Put the pizza base on a tray and spread with the onion mixture. Scatter the Feta cheese over and season. Bake for 10 minutes, then top with the prawns and cook for a further 5 minutes.

ITALIAN-STYLE RICE WITH LOTS OF PARMESAN

Risotto rice with lots of colour and flavour.

SERVES 4, PREP 10 MINS, COOKING 20 MINS

2 cloves garlic, peeled and crushed
50 g / 2 oz fresh mint leaves
25 g / 1 oz fresh basil leaves
1 tbsp hazelnuts
1 tbsp pine nuts
40 g / 1 1/2 oz Pecorino Romano or
Parmesan cheese, grated
100 ml / 3 1/2 fl oz extra virgin olive oil

250 ml / 8 fl oz arborio rice
500 ml / 16 fl oz boiling water
juice of 1 lime
sea salt flakes and ground black pepper
mint and basil leaves and Pecorino
Romano or Parmesan cheese shavings,
to garnish

Put the garlic, mint, basil, hazelnuts and pine nuts in a food processor and blend to a coarse paste. Stir in the cheese and season to taste. Gradually whisk in the oil. Put the rice in a large saucepan, add half of the mint mixture and mix to coat the grains. Pour the boiling water over the rice, bring back to the boil, cover and simmer for 20 minutes (add more water if necessary). Transfer to a serving bowl. Add the remaining mint sauce and the lime juice. Season to taste and leave to cool. When you are ready to eat, scatter the herbs and cheese shavings over the top.

BOMBAY POTATOES WITH BABY SPINACH

These potatoes may seem rather lonely, however I feel that they make a perfectly acceptable lunch in one pot if you put a few fresh spinach and rocket leaves underneath.

SERVES 4, PREP 15 MINS, COOKING 25 MINS

550 g / 1 1/4 lb potatoes
pinch of salt
1/2 tsp turmeric
4 tbsp vegetable oil
1/2 tsp ground coriander

1 tsp chilli powder
1/2 tsp garam masala (see page 16)
a big bunch of fresh spinach and rocket leaves, roughly torn

Boil the potatoes in their skins with the salt and turmeric for 5 minutes. Drain, allow to cool, peel and cut into chunks. Place the oil in a large frying pan or wok with the coriander and chilli powder and heat gently. As soon as the oil is hot, add the potatoes and stir well. Cover with a lid and leave to cook for 20 minutes, stirring occasionally. Add the garam masala and toss together, then continue to cook for a few more minutes. Divide a big bunch of fresh spinach and rocket leaves between four lunchboxes, top with the Bombay potatoes and serve.

PETIT POIS, SMOKED SALMON AND LINGUINE

I have used quite a lot of fresh fish, meat and chicken in this section so I decided to use some smoked salmon for a change. Having said that you could use fresh salmon if you prefer, or chicken or prawns for that matter.

SERVES 4, PREP 10 MINS, COOKING 12 MINS

450 g / 1 lb linguine
1 tbsp oil
1 shallot, peeled and sliced
125 g / 4 oz petit pois
300 ml / ½ pint double cream

a handful of fresh dill, roughly chopped
200 g / 7 oz smoked salmon, cut into thin strips
sea salt flakes and ground black pepper
2 lemons, cut into wedges

Bring a large pan of water to the boil and cook the pasta for 10–12 minutes; or until cooked but still al dente. Drain. Meanwhile, heat the oil in a frying pan, add the shallot and sauté for a few minutes. Add the petit pois, cream and dill, bring to the boil and simmer for 5 minutes. Add the smoked salmon and pasta, toss everything together and season to taste. Divide between four plates, or leave to cool and divide between four lunchboxes, scatter fresh dill over the top and serve with lemon wedges.

Balsamic and mustard chicken with roasted vegetables

Just imagine – slices of juicy chicken flavoured with balsamic vinegar and mustard mixed up with lots of chunky roasted vegetables and served with mayonnaise and hunks of bread!

Serves 4, Prep 15 mins (plus 30 mins marinating), Cooking 20 mins

FOR THE MARINADE
juice of 1 lemon
2 cloves garlic, peeled and finely chopped
1 tsp Dijon mustard
3 tbsp balsamic vinegar
3 tbsp olive oil
sea salt flakes and ground black pepper

4 chicken breasts

1 large aubergine, diagonally sliced
2 red peppers, peeled and seeded
2 yellow peppers, peeled and seeded
3 courgettes, diagonally sliced
2 red onions, peeled and cut into wedges
2 fennel bulbs, sliced into thin wedges
1 lemon, cut into wedges
mayonnaise and fresh bread, to serve

To make the marinade, mix together the ingredients in a small bowl, seasoning to taste.

Bash the chicken with a rolling pin, place in a shallow dish and pour the marinade over. Cover, refrigerate and leave for at least 30 minutes. Put all the vegetables in a bowl, add the oil and mix until evenly coated. Preheat the oven 180 °C / 350 °F / gas mark 4. Heat a griddle pan if you have one (it will give the food lovely criss-cross stripes) or use a heavy-based frying pan. Add the vegetables in batches to the hot griddle, sear on all sides, then transfer to an ovenproof dish. Once all the vegetables are slightly charred, add the chicken to the griddle and cook for 2 minutes on the top side. Place on top of the vegetables in the dish and cook in the preheated oven for 10 minutes or until the chicken is cooked. Serve immediately with lemon wedges, mayonnaise and fresh bread to mop up the chicken and vegetable juices.

SPICY SAUSAGES WITH BEANS

Golden onion, crispy bacon, juicy sausages and soft beans mixed together with fresh parsley and plenty of seasoning – delicious! You could make these into a baked bean-style dish by adding tinned tomatoes.

SERVES 4, PREP 10 MINS, COOKING 20 MINS

3 tbsp olive oil
2 cloves of garlic, peeled and finely chopped
2 large onions, peeled and sliced
6 rashers streaky bacon, sliced into little pieces

8 large herb sausages, roughly chopped
2 x 400 g / 14 oz cans cannellini beans, drained
3 tbsp flat leaf parsley, roughly chopped
sea salt flakes and ground black pepper

Heat the oil in a frying pan, add the garlic and onions and sauté for 10 minutes. Add the bacon and sausage pieces and continue to cook gently until they are cooked through. Add the beans and a little extra oil if wished and heat through. Stir in the parsley and season. Spoon on to four serving plates and serve, or leave to cool and take for lunch to reheat or eat cold.

SEARED BEEF WITH A PEPPER SAUCE

If you are short of time, pick up a pot of roasted peppers from the supermarket or local deli. If you are making this for one, just cook one steak and use the leftover pepper sauce for pasta or polenta. If you don't eat steak, cook chicken breasts or fish instead; the sauce tastes delicious with both.

SERVES 4, PREP 20 MINS, COOKING 35 MINS

2 red peppers, seeded
2 yellow peppers, seeded
2 tbsp olive oil
1 large onion, peeled and sliced

450 g / 1 lb plum tomatoes, seeded and chopped
4 x 125 g / 4 oz Scotch beef fillet

Put the peppers under a preheated grill for 30 minutes, turning occasionally, until black on all sides. Seal in a plastic bag and leave to sweat and cool for a few minutes. Peel away the skin, then seed and slice the flesh into strips. Heat half the oil in a large saucepan, add the onion and sauté for 2 minutes. Add the tomatoes and cook for a further 2 minutes. Heat a frying pan until really hot, add the remaining oil and heat. Add the steaks and sear for 2 minutes on each side to make them dark on the surface and pink and juicy in the middle. Slice the steaks. Add the pepper strips to the tomato mixture and season well. Serve the steak slices with the sauce or pack for lunch.

HERB NOODLES WITH TUNA

Keep it simple – it always works.

SERVES 4, PREP 10 MINS, COOKING 10 MINS

300 g / 11 oz noodles
50 g / 2 oz butter
1 small can tuna, drained
15 g / 1/2 oz mixed herbs such as
chervil, dill, parsley and oregano or a
bag of mixed fish herbs
sea salt flakes and ground black pepper

Cook the noodles in boiling water. Drain. Heat the butter in a frying pan, add the tuna, herbs and noodles, toss everything together and season to taste.

PAN-FRIED PRAWNS WITH AN ORANGE AND BASIL SAUCE

This is quite rich, but we need something rich every now and then. My mother very rarely used any butter or cream in her cooking, so I notice when dishes contain more than an ounce.

SERVES 4, PREP 15 MINS, COOKING 15 MINS

300 ml / 10 fl oz fish stock
50 ml / 2 fl oz dry vermouth
3 tbsp dry white wine
2 tbsp orange juice
150 g / 5 oz unsalted butter

1 tbsp olive oil
550 g / 1 1/4 lb fresh raw prawns
2 oranges, peeled and segmented
a handful of fresh basil, roughly torn
sea salt flakes and ground black pepper

Heat the stock, vermouth, wine and orange juice in a saucepan over a medium heat for 10 minutes until reduced by half. Meanwhile, melt 15 ml / 1 tbsp of the butter with the oil in a frying pan and cook the prawns for about 2 minutes on each side until cooked. Remove from the heat and keep warm. Dice the remaining butter. Remove the stock from the heat and quickly whisk in a piece of butter. Return the saucepan to a gentle heat and add the butter a piece at a time, whisking continuously. Stir in the orange segments and basil and season to taste. Serve the prawns in the sauce.

KEDGEREE

I am completely spoilt by living so close to Le Pont de La Tour's shop. It's a well-stocked store with amazing goodies. If I lack inspiration, I just pop in to see what's on offer and usually come away with at least one idea. Consequently, I couldn't resist asking the manager, Kirstine Spiers, for a recipe. If you are serving this at home, pile the kedgeree into a large heatproof serving dish, sprinkle over the Parmesan and brown under a hot grill for 5 minutes. Scatter over the fresh coriander and serve with crusty bread. Alternatively, leave to cool and take to work in a lunchbox, it travels really well.

SERVES 4, PREP 20 MINS, COOKING 35 MINS

1 litre / 1¾ pints milk
450 g / 1 lb Finnan haddock or other smoked fish fillet, skinned
1 tbsp olive oil
1 onion, peeled and chopped
2 garlic cloves, peeled and crushed
2 tsp curry paste

300 g / 11 oz arborio rice
1 litre / 1¾ pint vegetable stock
125 g / 4 oz Parmesan cheese
a handful of fresh coriander, roughly chopped
sea salt flakes and ground black pepper

Put the milk in a saucepan, bring to the boil, add the fish and turn off the heat. Leave to stand for 10 minutes or until the fish is cooked. Remove the fish from the milk, reserving the liquid, and flake the fish into large pieces and remove any bones. Heat the oil in a heavy-based saucepan and cook the onion and garlic for 10 minutes until soft and translucent but not browned. Add the curry paste and stir well. Cook for 1 minute. Add the rice and stir thoroughly for 2 minutes to make sure all the grains are coated in oil. Add a ladleful of the poaching liquid and allow it to be fully absorbed before adding another ladleful. Continue in this way, stirring constantly, until all the liquid is used up. At this point the rice will not be cooked but will begin to soften. Gradually add the vegetable stock and continue cooking for about 18 minutes until the rice is just cooked – you may not use all the stock. Remove from the heat and add all the flaked fish and half the Parmesan. Mix gently, scatter over the coriander and season to taste, cover and allow to stand for 5 minutes. Either serve warm with the remaining Parmesan or cool and then refrigerate before packing into lunchboxes.

SOMETHING SWEET

After a sandwich, salad or one-pot you may find yourself craving something sweet, so where would a lunchbox be without a few naughty but nice puds? Some days fresh fruit or a yoghurt is sufficient and other days it definitely is not! The best advice I can give is to have a batch of cookies or brownies in the freezer and to take them out for lunch one at a time – if you can be that restrained!

But if you're looking for an idea that is a little more exciting than fruit and yoghurt but just as healthy, you could make peppered poached pears, rhubarb compote with ginger shortbread, or oranges with lavender. However, my favourite sweets yet have got to be coconut rice pudding with mango, papaya and fresh basil and squillionaire's shortbread. Occasionally I will have a slice (or two) for lunch. I might even skip the sandwich first – it's a girl thing!

I know lots of people who run out of ideas for things to enjoy after their sandwiches. Layers of poached fruits in a pot with crunchy gingernut biscuits is so easy but a little more exciting. If you have a spare 10 minutes, make a batch of roasted cashew nut cookies, keep them in the freezer and just take one for lunch every now and then.

Get the children into the kitchen to make chocolate crispy cakes or lemon drizzle cakes for their packed lunches. Or you might fancy making a batch of muffins, fresh and soft for breakfast and delicious for lunch – they're unbelievably quick to make. The only thing to remember with muffins is that they are best on the day they're made. Freeze any that are left over and allow to thaw for 10 minutes before eating.

Those looking for a healthy lunch that is easy to eat on the run could make the muesli bars and eat a couple of slices with some fresh fruit.

The ideas are endless, especially if you adapt the fruit recipes to suit the season.

ROASTED CASHEW NUT COOKIES

I strongly advise you to roast any nuts before you use them in baking; it gives them a really intense flavour. These cookies freeze well and make a wonderful addition to any lunchbox.

MAKES 25, PREP 15 MINS, COOKING 10–15 MINS

125 g / 4 oz butter, plus extra for greasing
75 g / 3 oz light brown sugar
90 g / 3 1/2 oz golden granulated sugar
1 large egg
1 tbsp golden syrup

1/2 tsp vanilla essence
150 g / 5 oz plain flour
1/2 tsp baking powder
1/2 tsp salt
125 g / 4 oz cashew nuts, toasted

Preheat the oven to 190 °C / 375 °F / gas mark 5. Grease two baking sheets. Put the butter and sugars in a bowl and beat until light and fluffy. Beat in the egg, syrup and vanilla essence. Sieve the flour, baking powder and salt into the mixture. Add the nuts and fold everything together. Spoon 15 ml / 1 tbsp quantities of the mixture about 7.5 cm / 3 in apart on to the prepared baking sheets. Bake for 10–15 minutes or until golden brown. Leave to cool on the baking sheet for 5 minutes, then transfer to wire racks to cool completely.

POACHED FRUITS WITH RICOTTA CREAM

You'll be the envy of all your colleagues if you turn up to work with little pots of this for lunch. The combination of the creamy Ricotta and the poached fruits is a winner. I poach the fruits and keep a big bowl of them in the fridge to mix with yoghurt for supper, or to spoon on to hot muffins or, if I am out for the day, to take with me for lunch. If blackberries and plums are not in season, use other fruits instead.

SERVES 4, PREP 10 MINS, COOKING 25–30 MINS

125 g / 4 oz Ricotta cheese, softened
150 g / 4 oz natural Greek yoghurt
1 dtsp lemon juice
3 tbsp golden icing sugar

FOR THE POACHED FRUIT
75 g / 3 oz granulated sugar

250 ml / 9 fl oz water
250 g / 9 oz blackberries
8 plums, stoned and sliced
2 pieces of lemon rind
2 cloves
1/2 cinnamon stick

Mix together the Ricotta, yoghurt, lemon juice and icing sugar. Cover and refrigerate until needed.

To make the poached fruit, heat the sugar and water in a saucepan over a low heat until the sugar has dissolved, then add the fruit. Increase the heat and allow the syrup to boil for 5 minutes. Add the lemon rind, cloves and cinnamon and simmer slowly for 15 minutes or until the fruit is soft but not mushy.

Spoon the Ricotta mixture into one pot and the fruits into another and take both to work.

Peppered poached pears

Like the poached fruits recipe, this keeps very well in the fridge for a few days. Pop a poached pear into a container and take to work with a pot of yoghurt. They also look stunning on a picnic and travel really well.

Serves 4, Prep 15 mins, Cooking 35 mins

75 g / 3 oz golden caster sugar
568 ml / 1 pint red wine
100 ml / 3½ fl oz water

2 strips lemon rind
½ tbsp black peppercorns
4 large ripe pears

Put the sugar, wine, water, lemon rind and peppercorns into a saucepan and heat gently until the sugar dissolves, stirring occasionally. Bring to the boil. Meanwhile, peel the pears, leaving the stems, then core from the bottom of each without affecting the pear shape. Add the pears to the red wine mixture, bring to the boil and simmer gently for 25 minutes or until the pears are tender. Transfer the pears to four serving dishes, standing them upright. Return the liquid to the heat and boil, uncovered, for 10 minutes or until reduced to a syrup. Strain and spoon over the pears and decorate with a couple of peppercorns from the sauce (but it is best not to eat these).

CHOCOLATE CRISPY CAKES

A bit childish, but delicious and great fun for a lunchbox. Talking of children, why don't you get yours to help make these for their own mid-morning or lunchtime snacks?

Marshmallows, nuts, lumps of chocolate or other goodies could be added to the basic mix, if you are feeling adventurous.

MAKES 14, PREP 10 MINS, COOKING 5 MINS

200 g / 7 oz plain chocolate
2 tbsp golden syrup

50 g / 2 oz butter
50 g / 2 oz cornflakes

Put the chocolate, syrup and butter in a saucepan and melt gently over a low heat. Fold in the cornflakes and when mixed, divide between 14 paper cases. Leave to set.

SOFT FRUIT AND GINGERNUT LAYER

Other than poaching a few fruits very gently in a little brandy for few minutes, very little cooking is required for this recipe. If you are in a real hurry in the morning, make this dessert using fresh berries that do not require any cooking and layer with the yoghurt and biscuits. The muscovado sugar melts into the yoghurt, turning it into a caramel fudge-style cream.

SERVES 4, PREP 15 MINS, COOKING 5–10 MINS

3 peaches, stoned and sliced
3 apricots, stoned and sliced
3 nectarines, stoned and sliced
2 tbsp brandy or liqueur of your choice
65 ml / 2½ fl oz water

400 ml / 14 fl oz crème fraîche
400 ml / 14 fl oz Greek yoghurt
4 tbsp dark brown muscovado sugar
6 oz / 175 g thin gingernut biscuits, crushed

Gently heat the fruit, brandy and water in a saucepan for 5 minutes until the fruit is soft and the liquid has reduced. Remove from the heat and allow to cool. Mix together the crème fraîche and yoghurt and spoon 30 ml / 2 tbsp into the bottom of four glasses or pots if they need to be transported. Sprinkle a little of the sugar over the top, followed by some of the crushed biscuit and then some of the cooled fruit. Repeat the layers in each of the glasses, ending with fruit on the top. Chill for at least 30 minutes before serving.

Strawberry muffins

I just had to include some muffins in *Lunchbox*, all it takes is 10 minutes mixing time and 20 minutes baking time to whip out the freshest and tastiest muffins. If you are going to make the muffins at breakfast; weigh out the ingredients the night before, mix together the wet ingredients and the dry ingredients and keep in separate bowls overnight. In the morning, put the oven on, mix everything together and bake. Rising agents like baking powder have made it possible to make little muffins that rise in minutes, rather than the hours it takes a yeast dough to rise. Once all the ingredients are in the bowl, mix the muffin mixture really quickly because, unlike when we make cakes, we do not want to beat in lots of air. If the muffins are over-beaten, they will be tough when cooked. Muffins also freeze very well.

MAKES 30 MINI OR 12 LARGE, PREP 10 MINS, COOKING 15–20 MINS

140 g / 4 1/2 oz butter, melted
200 g / 7 oz plain flour
1 tbsp baking powder
125 g / 4 oz caster sugar
1/4 tsp ground cinnamon

a pinch of grated nutmeg
1/2 tsp salt
1 egg
175 ml / 6 fl oz milk
125 g / 4 oz strawberries, chopped

Preheat the oven to 220 °C / 425 °F / gas mark 7. Grease a mini or large muffin tray. Put the flour, baking powder, sugar, cinnamon, nutmeg and salt in a bowl, mix together and make a well in the centre. Mix together the egg, melted butter and milk and pour into the well with the strawberries. Very quickly stir with a wooden spoon just until mixed. Spoon into the prepared muffin tray and bake until golden for about 15 minutes if mini, 20 minutes if large.

BLUEBERRY AND BUTTERMILK MUFFINS

For full, beautifully rounded muffin tops, fill the cups all the way to the top. Use paper cases if you wish; they guarantee a muffin tray that is easy to clean and they help to keep the muffins separate from other food in the lunchbox. I have included some dried as well as fresh blueberries in this recipe for added flavour and sweetness and a contrast in texture. If you have other dried fruits that you wish to use instead of fresh (but you like the plumpness of fresh fruits), soak the dried fruits in fruit juice or liqueur first.

MAKES 12, PREP 15 MINS, COOKING 20 MINS

150 g / 5 oz unsalted butter, melted
and cooled
50 g / 2 oz golden caster sugar
2 eggs, beaten
250 ml / 9 fl oz buttermilk
2 teaspoons vanilla extract
400 g / 14 oz plain flour

a pinch of salt
1 tsp bicarbonate of soda
2 tsp baking powder
a pinch of grated nutmeg
125 g / 4 oz fresh blueberries, tossed
in 1 dtsp golden caster sugar
50 g / 2 oz dried blueberries

Preheat the oven to 200 °C / 400 °F / gas mark 6. Grease a tray of 12 muffin tins. Put the butter, sugar, eggs, buttermilk and vanilla into a bowl and mix well. Sieve the flour, salt, bicarbonate of soda, baking powder and nutmeg on to a plate. Add the dry ingredients and blueberries to the wet ingredients. Very quickly stir with a wooden spoon just until mixed. Do not beat. Spoon into the prepared muffin tray and bake for 20 minutes. Allow to cool before turning out.

BANANA AND BRAN MUFFINS

The success of this recipe depends on the ripeness of the bananas. You need the fruit to be really ripe so that the banana flavour is strong enough to come through the finished muffin. Don't panic if the mixture appears to be too thin – this is fine. Just get it straight into the tins and into the oven.

MAKES 12, PREP 20 MINS, COOKING 20–25 MINS

225 g / 8 oz bran cereal
175 g / 6 oz oat bran
225 g / 8 oz plain flour
2 tsp bicarbonate of soda
1 tsp ground cinnamon
a pinch of salt

2 eggs, beaten
250 ml / 9 fl oz buttermilk
75 ml / 3 fl oz honey
125 ml / 4 fl oz vegetable oil
2 large bananas or 3 small bananas, mashed

Preheat the oven to 200 °C / 400 °F / gas mark 6. Butter muffin tins or use paper cases. In a large bowl combine the bran, flour, bicarbonate, cinnamon and salt. In another bowl mix the beaten eggs, buttermilk, honey and oil. Add the mashed bananas, then add the wet ingredients to the dry ingredients. Mix well but do not beat. Divide into muffin tins. Bake for 20–25 minutes. To check that the muffins are ready, insert a toothpick into the centre of one; if it comes out clean, the muffins are done. Cool on a wire rack.

THE ULTIMATE CHOCOLATE BROWNIE

Any one who says they don't like chocolate is, in my opinion, not telling the truth. You may be thinking that a chocolate bar is easier and quicker to put into a lunchbox but bear in mind that these brownies are delicious as desserts served hot with cream, cold with a cup of tea or crumbly and moist for lunch with a coffee – after eating your sandwich, of course!

MAKES APPROX 16, PREP 15 MINS, COOKING 30 MINS

75 g / 5 oz unsalted butter
75 g / 7 oz plain chocolate
4 large eggs beaten
250 g / 12 oz soft brown sugar

1 tsp vanilla essence
150 g / 5 oz plain flour, sifted
1 tsp backing powder
a pinch of salt

Preheat the oven to 180 °C / 350 °F / gas mark 4. Grease a rectangular cake tin. Melt the butter and 75 g / 3 oz of the chocolate in a bowl over a pan of barely simmering water. Stir until smooth. Allow to cool slightly. Chop the remaining chocolate. Stir all the remaining ingredients and the chopped chocolate into the melted chocolate and blend thoroughly. Pour into the greased tin and bake for 30 minutes. It should still be squidgy in the middle. Cool in the tin for 10 minutes, then cut into squares and transfer to a wire rack to finish cooling.

CHOCOLATE FRIDGE CAKE

I call them cakes, even though you don't need to turn on the oven. You can also serve the squares with coffee after dinner instead of truffles.

MAKES 15 SLICES (APPROX.), PREP 15 MINS, COOKING 5 MINS

125 g / 4 oz butter
2 tbsp golden syrup
200 g / 7 oz dark chocolate, broken into pieces
225 g / 8 oz digestives, roughly crushed

50g / 2 oz walnuts
25g / 1 oz raisins
25g / 1 oz glacé cherries

Melt the butter and syrup in a saucepan. Take the pan off the heat, add the chocolate and stir until melted. Add the rest of the ingredients and mix thoroughly. Pour into a rectangular tin and leave in the fridge overnight to harden. Cut into squares and wrap in greaseproof paper for your lunchbox.

MUESLI SLICE WITH APRICOTS AND SUNFLOWER SEEDS

Any nuts and dried fruits can be used in this recipe, the one non-negotiable ingredient is *jumbo* oats. Their size really effects the finished texture of the slices.

MAKES 15, PREP 15 MINS, COOKING 20 MINS

150 g / 5 oz butter or margarine, plus extra for greasing
50 g / 2 oz golden caster sugar
125 g / 4 oz golden syrup
250 g / 9 oz jumbo rolled oats

25 g / 1 oz sunflower seeds or nuts
30 g / 1 oz chopped dried apricots
25 g / 1 oz raisins
1 tbsp sesame seeds

Preheat the oven to 180 °C / 350 °F / gas mark 4. Put the butter, sugar and syrup into a pan and heat until the butter is melted. Add all the other ingredients and mix well. Tip into a greased tin and bake for 20 minutes. Mark into squares and leave to cool in the tin. Cut and store in an airtight container.

CARAMELISED APPLE FLAPJACKS

These are such a treat to eat. Friends who adore flapjacks were adamant that the mixture should be kept plain and simple – until they tried this recipe. The caramelised apple makes the flapjacks really moist and succulent.

MAKES 10, PREP 15 MINS, COOKING 15–20 MINS

150 g / 5 oz butter, plus extra for greasing
3 Cox's apples

225 g / 8 oz golden caster sugar
2 tbsp lemon juice
275 g / 10 oz rolled oats

Preheat the oven to 200 °C / 400 °F / gas mark 6. Grease a square tin. Peel and core the apples and cut into small chunks. Melt the butter and sugar in a saucepan, then bring to bubbling point. Carefully add the apples and cook over a medium heat, stirring frequently, for about 8 minutes until caramelised. Carefully add the lemon juice (it will bubble furiously), then the oats and stir well. Pour into the prepared tin, and bake for 15–20 minutes. Mark into squares and leave to cool in the tin. Cut and store in an airtight container.

WHITE CHOCOLATE AND MACADAMIA NUT BLONDIES

This one is for *white* chocolate lovers. Try and use a good quality white chocolate with a high cocoa butter content. If there's not much cocoa butter the chocolate will be made up predominantly of vegetable fat and sugar.

MAKES 12, PREP 15 MINS, COOKING 25 MINS

150g / 5 oz unsalted butter, plus extra for greasing
400g/14 oz light muscavado sugar
1 tsp vanilla essence
3 large eggs, beaten
300g/11 oz plain flour

1 tsp baking powder
a pinch of salt
75g/3 oz macadamia nuts, roughly chopped
75g/3 oz white chocolate roughly chopped

Preheat the oven to 180 °C / 350 °F / gas mark 4. Melt the butter and sugar in a saucepan over a low heat. Allow to cool slightly, then stir in the vanilla and eggs. Sieve the flour, baking powder and salt into the pan and stir until just blended. Add the nuts and chocolate. Pour into a well greased rectangular tin and bake for 25 minutes. Leave to cool in the tin, then cut into squares and transfer to a wire rack to finish cooling.

LEMON DRIZZLE FAIRY CAKES

When I was nine years old I made – obviously for a price – what I called 'luscious lemon cakes' for all my mother's friends. My pocket money shot up very quickly. It was then that I knew I would always be involved with food. The reason I am including this recipe is because I learnt at that young age a very important trick in cake baking: drizzling icing over cakes while they are still warm creates a really luscious and moist end result. Prick a few holes in the cakes first to encourage the icing to drizzle right through to the centre. Try it and you will see exactly what I mean.

MAKES 12, PREP 10 MINS, COOKING 15–20 MINS

125 g / 4 oz butter
125 g / 4 oz golden caster sugar
2 eggs, beaten

125 g / 4 oz self raising flour
juice and finely grated rind of 2 lemons
75 g / 3 oz golden icing sugar

Preheat the oven to 190 °C / 375 °F / gas mark 5. Cream together the butter and sugar, add the eggs and sieve in the flour. Add half the lemon juice and rind and mix all together. Put spoonfuls of the mixture into paper cake cases and bake for 15–20 minutes. To make the icing, mix the remaining lemon rind and juice with the icing sugar and drizzle over the cakes while they are still warm. Leave the cakes to cool or eat them straight away.

CASHEW NUT GRANOLA

Granola is best described as a toasted muesli that is packed with flavour. It is the perfect thing to mix with natural yoghurts and poached or chopped fresh fruits. You could even use this as a crumble topping or on top of baked apples. So if you find yourself with a little time, make this mixture and keep it in a bag in the freezer for those occasions when you need to make a pudding quickly for lunch.

MAKES 10 PORTIONS (APPROX.), PREP 10 MINS, COOKING 35–45 MINS

350 g / 12 oz oats
50 g / 2 oz wheatgerm
50 g / 2 oz desiccated coconut
50 g / 2 oz sesame seeds
6 tbsp sunflower seeds
75 g / 3 oz cashews (or almonds)
175 ml / 6 fl oz oil

75 ml / 3 fl oz runny honey
1 tsp vanilla essence
1/4 tsp salt
125 g / 4 oz dried fruit such as apples, apricots, dates, prunes, raisins chopped into bite-sized pieces.

Preheat the oven to 150 °C / 300 °F / gas mark 2. Grease a rectangular tin. Mix together the oats, wheatgerm, coconut, sesame seeds, sunflower seeds and nuts in a large bowl. Combine the oil, honey, vanilla and salt in a large saucepan and cook over a gentle heat until the honey has melted. Pour the wet ingredients over the dry ingredients and mix thoroughly. Spread out the mixture in the tin. Bake for 35–45 minutes, stirring the mixture every 10 minutes. Allow to cool and add the dried fruit. Store in an airtight container.

PEAR AND BLACKBERRY CRISP

A crisp is the trendy (or modern) term for a crumble although, having said that, not all crumbles are crisp. Make this for supper and keep some for lunch. Spoon it into a pot and eat it cold with yoghurt or buy some ice cream.

SERVES 4, PREP 15 MINS, COOKING 30 MINS

700 g / 1 1/2 lbs pears
6 tbsp soft light brown sugar
225 g / 8 oz blackberries
65 g / 2 1/2 oz plain flour

1/2 tsp cinnamon
grating of nutmeg
a pinch of salt
75 g / 3 oz butter

Preheat the oven to 200 °C / 400 °F / gas mark 6. Peel and core the pears and put in a saucepan with 15 ml / 1 tbsp of the sugar and 15 ml / 1 tbsp water. Add the blackberries. Cook over a low heat for 3–4 minutes until the berry juice just begins to run. Tip into an ovenproof dish. Combine the flour, cinnamon, nutmeg and salt and the remaining sugar and rub in the butter until the mixture resembles fine breadcrumbs. Sprinkle over the fruit. Bake for 30 minutes.

CHOCOLATE CHIP COOKIES

These have been included due to popular demand. I must say that they freeze really well. Beware: they may not last in your lunchbox until lunchtime!

MAKES 12 (APPROX.), PREP 10 MINS, COOKING 8–10 MINS

350 g / 12 oz butter, plus extra for greasing
100 g / 3 1/2 oz sugar
200 g / 7 oz brown sugar
1 tsp vanilla essence
a pinch of salt

4 eggs, beaten
400 g / 14 oz plain flour
25 g / 1 oz cocoa powder
1/4 tsp bicarbonate of soda
175g / 6 oz chocolate chips

Preheat the oven to 180 °C / 350 °F / gas mark 4. Beat together the butter and sugars in a bowl until pale and fluffy. Add the vanilla, salt and eggs and mix together. Add the flour and bicarbonate of soda and blend to a smooth dough. Stir in the chocolate chips. Put teaspoonfuls on a greased baking sheet and bake for 8–10 minutes. Eat warm or transfer to a wire rack to cool.

SQUILLIONAIRE'S SHORTBREAD

If you are going to take this chocolate thing seriously, you need to pick up a pot of good quality cocoa. Dutch or French brands have an excellent flavour. Drinking chocolate will not work in the same way. Be careful not to overcook the biscuit base as it will turn bitter.

MAKES 15, PREP 25 MINS, COOKING 30 MINS (PLUS 2 HOURS BOILING TIME)

1 x 397 g / 14 oz tin condensed milk
225 g / 8 oz butter, plus extra for greasing
125 g / 4 oz golden caster sugar

25 g / 1 oz good quality cocoa
275 g / 10 oz plain flour
a pinch of salt
350 g / 12 oz dark chocolate

Put the unopened can of condensed milk in a saucepan, cover with water, bring to the boil and then simmer uncovered for 2 hours (keep topping up with water so that the can remains covered). Leave the can to cool completely before opening (this is important). The condensed milk will have turned into a fudgy golden caramel.

Preheat the oven to 180 °C / 350 °F / gas mark 4. Grease a deep 20 x 28 cm / 8 x 11 in cake tin. Beat the butter until soft, add the sugar and mix until light and fluffy. Sieve in the cocoa, flour and salt. Use your hands to bring the ingredients quickly together to make a dough. Press the dough into the prepared cake tin. Prick all over with a fork. Bake for 30 minutes until just firm and darkening very slightly around the edges. Leave to cool. When cold, spoon the caramel over the shortbread and refrigerate for about 1 hour until firm. Melt the chocolate in a bowl over a pan of gently simmering water. Pour the melted chocolate evenly over the caramel. When the chocolate is almost set but still slightly soft, cut the shortbread into squares.

SOUR CREAM AND CINNAMON SCONES

If you don't really have a sweet tooth, or you just fancy something that is not as rich or sweet as the chocolate recipes, this one is for you. When I tested this recipe, I ate some, put the rest in a bag and into my freezer and I have been eating them at all times of the day ever since. They have so much flavour that you don't really need to serve them with anything else. However, for breakfast they are delicious smothered in butter and runny honey and for lunch they are wonderful with cream cheese.

SERVES 4, PREP 10 MINS, COOKING 12–14 MINS

200 g / 7 oz self-raising flour
1/2 tsp baking powder
1 tsp ground cinnamon
a pinch of sea salt flakes
1 tbsp golden caster sugar, a little extra
for sprinkling

4 tbsp sour cream
1 medium egg
75 ml / 3 fl oz milk

Preheat the oven to 220 °C / 425 °F / gas mark 7. Sieve the flour, baking powder, cinnamon and salt into a bowl. Stir in the sugar and make a well in the centre. In a separate bowl, mix together the soured cream, egg and milk and pour into the well in the dry ingredients. Mix everything together but do not beat. Drop 10 little spoonfuls on to a baking sheet, sprinkle with a little extra sugar and bake for 12–14 minutes until golden brown and cooked through.

COCONUT RICE PUDDING WITH TROPICAL FRUITS AND BASIL

A taste of the tropics in every mouthful. This looks stunning and tastes as indulgent as any rice pudding but without the fat! You really do need to use pudding rice. Save the seeds from the pawpaw and use them in a salad dressing, they are really peppery and very good for the digestion.

This pudding is delicious cold, thinned with a little crème fraîche or yoghurt.

SERVES 4, PREP 15 MINS, COOKING 20 MINS

150 g / 5 oz pudding rice
250 ml / 8 1/2 fl oz full-cream milk
250 ml / 8 1/2 fl oz coconut milk
100 ml / 3 1/2 fl oz water
1/2 tsp vanilla essence

25 g / 1 oz golden caster sugar
1 large ripe mango
1 large ripe papaya
a handful of fresh basil leaves, roughly torn, to serve

Put the rice, milk, coconut milk, water and vanilla in a saucepan and stir. Bring to the boil, reduce the heat and simmer for 15–20 minutes, stirring frequently to prevent it from sticking on the bottom. If necessary, add a few tablespoons of water to loosen the mixture. Add the sugar, mix well and cook for 1 minute. Halve the mango widthways, twist the halves and remove the stone. Peel and slice the flesh. Seed the papaya, peel and slice the flesh. Arrange the fruits on four large serving plates and spoon a little rice pudding next to the fruits. Scatter a few basil leaves over the top and serve. For a lunchbox, leave the pudding to cool, put into a pot, top with the fruits and basil and away you go.

SPICED APPLE SAUCE

This is low in calories and fat – in fact I haven't added any fat at all. This is perfect with yoghurt or crème fraîche and granola, and who said puddings take time to make?

SERVES 4, PREP 10 MINS, COOKING 5–10 MINS

8 Cox's apples, peeled, cored and cut into chunks
450 ml / 15 fl oz apple juice
1 tsp minced root ginger
1 1/2 tsp ground cinnamon
1/2 tsp allspice
1/2 tsp cloves
1 star anise
lemon juice to taste

Put all the ingredients in a large heavy-based saucepan. Heat gently over a medium heat for about 5–10 minutes until the apples are tender. Mash with a potato masher to the texture you want.

RHUBARB COMPÔTE WITH GINGER SHORTBREAD

Rhubarb goes really well with both orange and ginger, so I have added orange juice to the fruit and ginger to the shortbread. Be careful not to overcook the fruit; it will go mushy if left in the oven too long. This recipe is written to serve four people, but if you have more than 450 g / 1 lb of rhubarb, cook it all at the same time and keep it in the freezer to serve with yoghurts and/or granola. If you decide not to make the shortbread, but still wish to make the compôte, cook the fruits in a saucepan on the hob, instead. This shortbread can be stored in an airtight container.

SERVES 4, PREP 15 MINS, COOKING 30–35 MINS

FOR THE GINGER SHORTBREAD
50 g / 2 oz preserved ginger
150 g / 5 oz butter
100 g / 3 1/2 oz golden icing sugar, sieved
100 g / 3 1/2 oz plain flour, sieved

FOR THE RHUBARB COMPÔTE
450 g / 1 lb rhubarb
juice of 1 large orange
golden caster sugar, to taste

To make the shortbread, chop the ginger into fine matchsticks. Beat the butter in a bowl with a wooden spoon to soften. Add the remaining ingredients and mix well. The mixture will be sticky. Put into a rectangular cake tin and prick with a fork. Bake for 30–35 minutes. Transfer to a wire rack to cool.

To make the compôte, chop the rhubarb into chunks, put into an ovenproof dish and pour over the orange juice and sugar to taste. Cover with foil and bake for 10–15 minutes alongside the shortbread. Serve little pots of the rhubarb compôte warm or at room temperature with the ginger shortbread for dipping.

QUICK TIRAMISU

Try to make this up the night before you are going to eat it to allow the flavours to develop. If you can resist this until lunchtime, you are a saint.

SERVES 4, PREP 15 MINS (PLUS UP TO 8 HOURS CHILLING TIME)

10 sponge fingers
100 ml / 3¹/₂ fl oz very strong coffee
4 tbsp Marsala
2 eggs, separated

25 g / 1 oz golden caster sugar
225 g / 8 oz Mascarpone cheese
50 g / 2 oz dark chocolate, grated for sprinkling OR cocoa powder to dust

Put the sponge fingers in a serving bowl. Mix together the coffee and Marsala and pour over the sponge fingers, making sure they are thoroughly soaked. Whisk together the egg yolks and sugar until thick and creamy, then whisk in the Mascarpone. In a separate bowl whisk the egg whites until stiff, then fold into the Mascarpone mixture using a metal spoon. Pour over the sponge fingers. Sprinkle over the grated chocolate or dust liberally with cocoa powder. Refrigerate for as long as possible, preferably overnight, before serving.

ALMOND FUDGEY BITES

Simply scrummy with ice cream or crème fraiche or on their own. These nutty bites are quite chewy, nutty, and fudgey all at the same time.

SERVES 4, PREP 10 MINS, COOKING 15 MINS

125 g / 4 oz ground almonds
75 g / 3 oz soft brown sugar

2 large egg whites
1/2 tsp vanilla essence

Preheat the oven to 180 °C / 350 °F/ gas mark 4. Line three baking sheets with baking parchment. Mix together the almonds and sugar thoroughly. Whisk together the egg whites and vanilla until stiff and glossy. Add the nut mixture to the egg whites and fold in until evenly blended. Spoon 10 ml / 1 dtsp quantities of the mixture on to the parchment, leaving space between them so they can expand slightly. Bake for 15–20 minutes until golden and slightly firm. Allow to cool slightly on the baking sheets, then lift off the paper and leave to cool completely. Store in an airtight container.

GREEK YOGHURT WITH PEACHES AND CRUSHED AMARETTI

More of an idea than a recipe. Use more or less of each ingredient to make it exactly how you wish.

SERVES 4, PREP 10 MINS

3 ripe peaches
1 tbsp lemon juice

1 small pot of Greek yoghurt
8 amaretti biscuits, roughly crushed

Put the peaches in a bowl, pour over boiling water and leave for 1 minute. Drain. Slip off the skins. Slice the fruit into a bowl and pour over the lemon juice. Layer the yoghurt, peach slices and amaretti in four small dishes or containers. Leave for a couple of hours or overnight before eating.

ORANGES WITH LAVENDER

Lavender is becoming more popular as a culinary herb. It adds a very subtle sweet perfume and flavour to this dessert.

SERVES 4, PREP 20 MINS (PLUS CHILLING TIME)

4 large oranges
4 blood oranges or minneolas
juice of 1 lemon

1 tbsp dried lavender, picked through for any bits

On a chopping board peel the oranges with a sharp serrated knife following the curve of the fruit, making sure you remove all the bitter white pith. Slice the fruits into rounds or chunks as you prefer, removing any pips as you go. Put the fruit into a bowl and pour over the lemon juice. Sprinkle the lavender over and mix thoroughly but gently. Refrigerate for a couple of hours, then allow the dish to come to room temperature before serving.

ETON MESS

Nothing new about this version of a particular old favourite, but I feel this book should contain recipes that everyone loves and enjoys. Use other fruits if you prefer. As long as the fruit is dry (not wet, if washed) and the meringue pieces are not too small, the mixture should keep quite happily in the fridge for a good few hours.

SERVES 4, PREP 15 MINS

225 g / 8 oz strawberries   225 g / 8 oz meringue
200 ml / 8 fl oz double cream

Wash and hull the strawberries. Cut them in half. Whip the cream until it forms soft peaks. Quickly fold in the meringue and fruit, taking care not to overwhip the cream. Refrigerate until you want to eat it.

HOMEMADE LEMONADE

Very easy, and it makes a nice change to the often artificial-tasting lemonades that you can buy in the shops.

SERVES 4, PREP 10 MINS

3 lemons

1 lime

175 g / 6 oz golden caster sugar

900 ml / 1 1/2 pints boiling water

Remove the lemon and lime rind with a sharp knife or a potato peeler, being careful to avoid any of the bitter white pith. Put the rind and sugar in a bowl or jug and pour over the boiling water. Cover and leave to cool, stirring occasionally. Squeeze the lemons and add the juice to the water. Strain the drink and refrigerate.

MANGO AND COCONUT SMOOTHIE

Coconut and mango is a delicious combination and the lime cuts through the flavour so that it is not too sweet. The beauty of this smoothie is that it travels really well, so you can make it and take it in a thermos flask to the pitch for half time!

SERVES 4, PREP 10 MINS

2 large ripe mangoes
400 ml / 14 oz can coconut milk

juice of 1 lime
crushed ice

Halve the mangoes widthways, twist the halves and pull apart. Cut around the stone left on one half to release the flesh and pull it out. Scoop out the flesh into a food processor, add the coconut milk and lime juice and whiz until smooth and frothy. Serve on lots of crushed ice.

PINEAPPLE, PINK GRAPEFRUIT AND PASSION FRUIT SMOOTHIE

Both of the smoothie recipes in this book are suitable for people with dairy allergies. This fruity number is packed with vitamins. If you really don't like the look of passion fruit pips, sieve the juice from the fruit and throw away the seeds.

SERVES 4, PREP 10 MINS

2 x 340 g / 12 oz packs prepared fresh pineapple chunks or equivalent weight of fresh pineapple fruit

600 ml / 1 pint freshly squeezed pink grapefruit
6 passion fruit

Whiz the pineapple in a blender or food processor until smooth, add the grapefruit juice, mix together and pour into a jug. Halve the passion fruits, scoop the juice and pips into the pineapple mixture, mix together and serve.

INDEX

25